THE HOME GUARD TRAINING POCKET MANUAL

THE HOME GUARD TRAINING POCKET MANUAL

Edited by Lee Johnson

CASEMATE

Oxford & Philadelphia

Published in Great Britain and
the United States of America in 2019 by
CASEMATE PUBLISHERS
The Old Music Hall, 106–108 Cowley Road, Oxford OX4 1JE, UK
1950 Lawrence Road, Havertown, PA 19083, USA

Introduction and chapter introductory texts by Lee Johnson
© Casemate Publishers 2019

Hardback Edition: ISBN 978-1-61200-7670
Digital Edition: ISBN 978-1-61200-7687

A CIP record for this book is available from the British Library

Printed in the Czech Republic by FINIDR, s.r.o.

Typeset in India by Versatile PreMedia Services. www.versatilepremedia.com

The information and advice contained in the documents in this book is solely
for historical interest and does not constitute advice. The publisher accepts no
liability for the consequences of following any of the advice in this book.

For a complete list of Casemate titles, please contact:

CASEMATE PUBLISHERS (UK)
Telephone (01865) 241249
Fax (01865) 794449
Email: casemate-uk@casematepublishers.co.uk
www.casematepublishers.co.uk

CASEMATE PUBLISHERS (US)
Telephone (610) 853-9131
Fax (610) 853-9146
Email: casemate@casematepublishers.com
www.casematepublishers.com

CONTENTS

Introduction   7

Chapter 1
The Object of the Home Guard   17

Chapter 2
Organisation   29

Chapter 3
Arms Drill   41

Chapter 4
Field Exercises   49

Chapter 5
Rifles and Rifle Shooting   69

Chapter 6
Small Arms   81

Chapter 7
Hand Grenades   143

Chapter 8
Night Fighting   149

Sources   159

INTRODUCTION

Mention the British Home Guard and, in most cases, the mental image that will spring to mind is of David Croft and Jimmy Perry's wonderful TV sitcom *Dad's Army* of the late 1960s and 1970s – Captain Mainwaring and the gallant, if mostly aged, men of the Walmington-on-Sea Platoon willing to lay down their lives to foil the dastardly 'Hun'. The passage of time and the historical knowledge that Nazism was defeated allows us to look back on this period of British history with fondness and humour but the origins of the Home Guard lay in very dark days indeed when Britain fought on alone against a triumphant Nazi Germany to prevent the world sinking 'into the abyss of a new Dark Age'.

On 10 May 1940 the Germans launched *Fall Gelb* (Operation *Yellow*), the invasion of the Netherlands, Belgium and France. In a textbook *blitzkrieg* campaign, the Allied forces were out-thought, out-manoeuvred and outflanked. By 13 May, the Germans were across the Meuse River at Sedan and a week later they reached the Channel coast at Abbeville. Within weeks, Britain faced an enemy-occupied coastline from the Franco-Spanish border to the North Cape. The threat of invasion was real and imminent.

Discussions around the idea of raising some sort of home defence force had been taking place in official circles from the very outbreak of war, but the origins of the World War II Home Guard can be traced back to Captain Tom Wintringham's 1939 book *How to Reform the Army*. Wintringham had fought with International Brigades in Spain against Franco's Fascists, rising to command the British 16th Battalion. In his book, Wintringham called for 100,000 men to be trained and organised into 12 divisions, organised along similar lines to the International Brigades, to help resist any invasion. Despite considerable War Office interest in the book, Wintringham's ideas were never pursued, partly as a result of official suspicions of Wintringham's Communist Party connections. Nevertheless, by October 1939 First Sea Lord, Winston Churchill, was calling for the forming of a Home Guard force of 500,000 men.

Six months later, after the disastrous Norwegian campaign, Neville Chamberlain resigned and Churchill became prime minister on the day the German forces launched their invasion of the West. On the evening of Tuesday 14 May 1940, Sir Anthony Eden, Secretary of State for War, made a radio broadcast calling for large numbers of British subjects between the ages of 17 and 65 to come forward to form what were to be called the Local Defence Volunteers. It was anticipated that around 500,000 volunteers might answer the call but by July the number stood at three times that. Existing stocks of uniforms and weaponry were largely earmarked for re-equipping and expanded the regular forces and despite Eden's assurances that 'you will not be paid, but you will receive uniform and will be armed', this promise proved impossible to keep in the short term.

Planning had been hurried and muddle and duplication characterised the administration's initial efforts to organise the force. The failure to issue proper uniforms or weapons, which simply did not exist at this juncture, led to resentment and impatience. The sense of indignation was beautifully articulated in Noel Coward's 1941 song *Could you please oblige us with a Bren Gun?* in which the protagonist, Colonel Montmorency, points out 'with the vicar's stirrup pump, a pitchfork and a spade it's rather hard to guard an aerodrome, so if you can't oblige us with a Bren Gun, the Home Guard might as well go home.' On 22 July, the new force's name was changed to the 'Home Guard' at Churchill's insistence, despite 1,000,000 'LDV' armbands having already been printed. The Home Guard remained poorly armed and

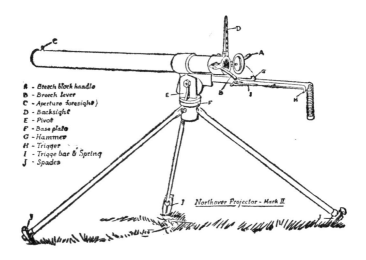

A - Breech block handle
B - Breech lever
C - Aperture foresight)
D - Backsight
E - Pivot
F - Base plate
G - Hammer
H - Trigger
I - Trigge bar & Spring
J - Spades

Northover Projector - Mark II

Illustration of a Northover projector from *Home Guard Proficiency* by John Brophy. The creation of a Home Guard officer, Robert Northover, it was supplied to Home Guard units as a stop-gap anti-tank weapon from late 1940. Its effective range was between 100 and 150 yards and it was cheap to manufacture. It was heavy and cumbersome and the No. 76 phosphorus grenades tended to break in the breech damaging the gun and injuring the crew.

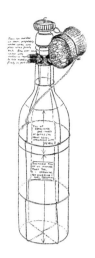

IIllustration of a Molotov cocktail from *Home Guard Pocket Book* by Brig-Gen. A. F. U. Green. An illustration from an extract on 'Molotov Bottles' written by P. W. Felton of the Steyning Home Guard. Green was a volunteer with the West Sussex Home Guard and published his pocket book early in the war when this sort of improvised grenade may have been all that was available to many units.

equipped for the first few weeks of its existence. Although orders were placed for Ross rifles from Canada and M1917 Enfields from the USA, for the time being volunteers relied on a mixture of sporting rifles, shotguns, ex-officer's personal sidearms and World War I souvenirs. Some Home Guard units even resorted to raiding museums for firearms. By late 1940 more than 700,000 volunteers remained unarmed and when Churchill wrote to the War Office in June 1941 insisting that 'every man must have a weapon of some sort, be it only a mace or pike' there had been no significant improvement. Their response was well-intentioned but insensitive. An order was placed for 250,000 'Croft's pikes', a length of steel tubing with a bayonet welded to the end. When these first reached the Home Guard, the response was, understandably, fury. In the House of Commons, Captain Godfrey Nicholson MP summed up the feeling when he said the issue of the pikes 'if not meant as a joke, was an insult.' As supplies of firearms became more available, Home Guard armament improved, in particular 500,000 of the M1917 Enfield, more accurate and powerful, if heavier, than the SMLE issued to the regulars. These were supplemented by supplies of M1918 Browning Automatic Rifles, Thompson submachine guns and, from early 1942, Sten submachine guns.

Nevertheless, there was a considerable amount of improvisation and a number of outdated weapons were passed on to the Home Guard by the regulars. Training manuals provided detailed instructions on how to make weapons such as the satchel charge and the 'Molotov cocktail' – an improvised incendiary weapon consisting of a glass bottle filled with a mixture of tar, Creosote and petrol. First used by Republican forces in the Spanish Civil War, it did not receive its popular moniker until the Russo-Finnish Winter War of 1939 when the Finns used them to knock out hundreds of Red Army tanks.

The Home Guard also received quantities of 'Heath-Robinson' weaponry whose existence was due only to the critical shortages resulting from the disastrous losses during the French campaign and the Dunkirk evacuation. These included the Northover projector, designed by Robert Northover, a Home Guard officer, the Smith Gun and the Blacker Bombard, all makeshift anti-tank weapons. Often put into production at Churchill's personal insistence, these weapons were regarded by the regular army as largely ineffective, unreliable or downright dangerous. Passed to Home Guard units, they remained in service until replaced by more effective weapons such as the 2-pdr. anti-tank gun. Another weapon issued to the Home Guard in considerable quantities was the anti-tank hand grenade No. 74, more commonly known as the ST grenade or sticky bomb. The grenade consisted of a sphere of nitroglycerin covered in a layer of strong adhesive that gave the grenade its name. Pulling a pin on the handle released the metal casing that covered the sticky head of the grenade. Pulling a second pin armed the grenade and the soldier would then attach the grenade to the enemy vehicle, the five-second fuse activated by a lever when the handle was released. The sticky bomb did not perform well in tests, proving as happy to stick to a uniform as to an enemy vehicle. In addition, it was difficult to attach the grenade to a vehicle that was heavily covered in dust or mud. The grenade was not approved for use by the British Army but, once again, Churchill intervened and some 2,500,000 were manufactured between 1940 and 1943, the vast majority issued to Home Guard units.

The composition of the Home Guard has always been characterised as primarily men too old to serve in the armed forces. It is undoubtedly true that veterans played a significant role in the Home Guard and many of its officers were ex-regular army who had seen action on the Western Front or in other active theatres. The popular TV series *Dad's Army* may well have played a part in reinforcing the prejudice that the Home Guard was made up of the superannuated with a smattering of 'stupid boys'. The reality seems to have been very different, however. A study of documents released by the National Archives in 2012 revealed that around half of the 4,000,000 men who served between 1940 and 1945 were under 27 and a third were under 18. Far from being an all-inclusive body that anyone could volunteer

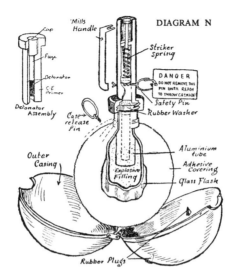

Illustration of an ST grenade, or sticky bomb, from *Home Guard Proficiency* by John Brophy. The sticky bomb was first issued to Home Guard units in 1940 and despite its flaws seems to have been adopted with some affection.

for, studies by Professor Penny Summerfield and Corinna Peniston-Bird, published in *Contesting Home Defence: men, women and the Home Guard in the Second World War*, show that recruitment practices were much more selective than the official line indicated. Indeed, there was heavy criticism from some of those not allowed to join. The documents are worthy of further study but they suggest that the men of the Home Guard were significantly more robust and formidable than the depiction of Captain Mainwaring's Walmington-on-Sea Platoon would have us believe.

The early months of the existence of the Home Guard were marked by considerable controversy and argument about the role that this new force would actually play in the defence of the realm. The War Office and the army were clear that, given its lack of weapons, equipment and training, the Home Guard should maintain a passive role as an armed constabulary. In the case of an invasion, it would observe German troop movements, passing information on to the regular army and occupying or guarding important locations, manning road blocks but would play no active role in the nation's defence. This again caused resentment and anger in the ranks of the Home Guard who felt that they were perfectly capable and indeed well-suited to an active role hunting down parachutists, saboteurs and fifth columnists as well as attacking German airborne landings and harassing and delaying other German units. Complaints were made to the War Office and the official positions did soften. Training manuals make it clear that within a matter of months Home Guard training explicitly encouraged the active engagement of enemy units where practical. Churchill was explicit on the subject. The active resistance of any Nazi invasion was the duty of each and every subject. Home Guard volunteers remained, legally, civilians unless officially ordered to muster by the Commander-in-Chief, Home Forces in the case of invasion. The British Government was explicit that Home Guard service should only be carried out in approved uniform and maintained that uniformed volunteers were lawful combatants under the terms of the Geneva Conventions. Whether, in the case of an invasion, the German armed forces would have recognised them as such is open to debate. Certainly, German radio broadcasts consistently referred to the Home Guard as 'gangs of murderers' and the conduct of German troops in the Balkans and Russia, where captured partisans, uniformed or not, were shot out of hand, suggests not.

Responsibility for the vast bulk of Home Guard training fell on the units themselves at a local level. The popularity of the numerous manuals and pamphlets published during the war, both official and privately produced, is testament to the appetite for information to support training. There were both private and official efforts to provide more formalised training to the Home Guard. At Osterley Park in southwest London a private training camp for the Home guard was opened in early 1940, funded by Edward Hulton, the magazine publisher. Tom Wintringham, a World War I veteran and former commander of the British Battalion of the 15th International Brigade in Spain, trained Home Guard volunteers in guerrilla-style warfare. Several other veterans who had fought for the Republic in Spain worked as instructors at Osterley, including Bert 'Yank' Levy. Osterley Park was closed after three months, partly as a result of suspicion of Tom Wintringham's former communist connections. Indeed, in *Contesting Home Defence* Penny Summerfield and Corinna Peniston-Bird state, 'the Osterley Park experiment is usually seen as a daring attempt by the Left to train a citizens' guerrilla army, inspired by ex-communist firebrand Wintringham, and stamped on by the authorities' but as they point out, the situation was more complex. Far from suppressing the school at Osterley, the War Office absorbed it into its own training system. The 'new' school opened two weeks later in the grounds of another large country house, 'Denbies' in Surrey, taught a very similar syllabus and retained several of Osterley's personnel including both Levy and Wintringham.

Indeed, despite Osterley Park challenging its orthodoxy, another such camp was also approved at Burwash in Sussex. In December 1941, Burwash was officially recognised as the South-Eastern Command Fieldcraft Training School. John Langdon-Davies, Home Guard captain and author of numerous

A self-portrait of Alfred E. Kerr taken from his manual *The Art of Night Fighting*. Kerr drew this likeness in September 1939 while on active service with 1st Battalion, London Irish Rifles. He wrote numerous manuals of instruction for the Home Guard and his opinions often challenged accepted military orthodoxy.

training manuals, was its commandant and, although more acceptable to the establishment, not having Wintringham's communist connections – Langdon-Davies had reported from the Republican side in Spain – Burwash taught similar guerrilla tactics to Osterley.

The plethora of material published during the war, including official War Office publications and privately published books, manuals and pamphlets served a number of purposes. The most obvious was to pass on expertise and skills to allow the Home Guard to improve its discipline, professionalism and tactical acumen. It is clear that another explicit desire was to pass on hard lessons learned during the current conflict. In the same way that Tom Wintringham and John Langdon-Davies sought to draw on the lessons of their experiences with the Republican forces in the Spanish Civil War, men like John Brophy and Alfred Kerr drew lessons from the campaigns in Norway and France and, as the war continued from Crete, the Balkans and Russia. It was clear that German successes in Norway, Holland, Belgium and France had depended heavily on surprise and speed of movement. Training materials, whilst acknowledging that it was not the role of the Home Guard to directly engage the enemy's main force, did seek to demonstrate how the Home Guard could harass and delay the progress of an invasion force and to point out the opportunities that might present themselves to attack disorganised or fragmented enemy units and to pick off stragglers. In Holland and Belgium and again in Crete in May 1941, airborne forces played a crucial role in seizing key points during the early hours of the invasion. These forces had been shown to be vulnerable in the first few minutes after landing, particularly if they struggled to reach the weapons canisters dropped with them. Home Guard training emphasised the need to respond swiftly and aggressively to any airborne landing in their area.

Interestingly, in this case the Germans and Allies learned opposite lessons from the same experiences. Heavy casualties amongst the *Fallschirmjäger*, particularly in the Crete fighting, left Hitler unwilling to commit to large-scale airborne landings with German airborne forces operating more as elite infantry units for the remainder of the war. The Allies, meanwhile, had been impressed by the performance of the German airborne troops and in particular their ability to seize key strategic points ahead of advancing ground troops. They developed their own airborne forces and employed them extensively during the 1944–45 campaign in Northwest Europe but, again, often at heavy cost.

One other impact of the numerous training publications, implicit, if not explicit, in much of the writing, is the intended effect on the morale of the Home Guard. This force was a unique experiment, neither a citizen militia nor yet a regular military force, its role initially contentious and unclear and indeed its competence challenged in official circles. Its ranks contained an amalgam of untrained novices with no military experience whatsoever and veterans, many of whom would have been aware that the tactics of their generation had been swept away by a new type of warfare. The emphasis on 'pluck', 'improvisation' and a 'have-a-go' attitude in much of the writing often reads, to the modern eye, more like propaganda than training but it was undoubtedly intended to give the Home Guard members who read it, and who were trained by those who read it, a sense of purpose and confidence and that, if called upon, they were capable and competent to do their duty effectively.

This is in no way to belittle the genuine improvements made. The level of Home Guard training undoubtedly improved as the war went on, as did its weapons and equipment, and by 1944 the force was unrecognisable from the ad-hoc 'broomstick army' of the LDV of June 1940. The force's role changed as well. Having crushed France, Hitler now planned the invasion of Britain – Operation *Sealion*. The failure of the Luftwaffe to overcome 'The

Few' of the RAF or to establish air superiority over the Channel during the Battle of Britain in the summer and autumn of 1940, meant the immediate threat of invasion receded, a fact acknowledged by Churchill in his speech to the House of Commons on 5 November 1940. The Home Guard now began to take on other, wider duties, guarding key facilities such as factories, airfields, bridges and oil refineries. In addition, they began to man anti-aircraft batteries and coastal artillery batteries. All these roles were designed to release regular army formations for combat duties. As a result of the heavy German bombing campaigns of 1940 and 1941, the Home Guard also took on a new role, that of locating unexploded bombs, sealing off the area and evacuating civilians. It was in carrying out this role that most wartime Home Guard casualties were suffered. The German invasion of the Balkans and then the Soviet Union in 1941 showed that Hitler's eye had turned eastward. Nevertheless, a very genuine fear of a German invasion remained and it was not until the tide on the Eastern Front turned decisively against the Germans in 1943, that the need for the Home Guard began to diminish. Even then the Home Guard continued to play an important security role allowing the regular forces to concentrate on preparations for the opening of the second front in Europe. With the D-Day landings and the subsequent successful breakout of the Allied forces across France and Belgium, the serious threat of German invasion receded and the Home Guard was stood down on 3 December 1944. It was finally disbanded following the end of the war on 31 December 1945.

Argument continues as to the effectiveness of the Home Guard. Thankfully, it was never called upon to fulfil the role for which it was formed, helping to repel a full-scale German invasion of Britain. Given the parlous state of the regular army in the summer of 1940 the outcome of any invasion must have been in doubt but the argument as to what that result would have been and the Home Guard's military success or otherwise in that is almost entirely academic. What is undeniable is that, at its peak, more than 1,700,000 men served in the Home Guard carrying out a huge range of tasks from guarding factories and airfields to manning anti-aircraft guns. The Home Guard was credited with downing a number of German aircraft and V1 flying bombs, their first confirmed 'kill' being over Tyneside in 1943. It was transformed from a poorly equipped, poorly armed and poorly trained mass in June 1940 to a force capable of taking over many of the defensive duties of the regular army by 1944. General Sir John Burnett-Stuart, commander of the 1st Aberdeen Battalion characterised the Home Guard as 'the outward and visible sign of the spirit of resistance.'

I have left the last word on the 'faithful, unwearying and absolutely indispensable work done by the Home Guard' to Britain's wartime prime minister. In a speech broadcast from the White House on 14 May 1943 to mark the third anniversary of the Home Guard's formation, Churchill said, 'We must not overlook or consider as matters of mere routine, those unceasing daily and nightly efforts of millions of men and women which constitute the foundation of our capacity to wage this righteous war wherever it may carry us all over the world.'

CHAPTER I
THE OBJECT OF THE HOME GUARD

The first two chapters of this book are excerpts from the October 1942 edition of *The Home Guard Training Manual* written by Major John Langdon-Davies who at the time was Commandant of the South Eastern Command Fieldcraft School at Burwash. Langdon-Davies had reported on the Spanish Civil War for the *News Chronicle*, where he had expressed admiration for the Anarchists but felt their militias were incapable of mounting an effective defence against Franco's Nationalists. This undoubtedly influenced his writings on the role of the Home Guard, as did the events of the first ten months of the war. The rapidity with which the defence of both the Low Countries and France collapsed in the face of the Wehrmacht's *blitzkrieg* tactics came as a profound shock. It took German forces just ten days to reach the Channel coast.

The Home Guard was never intended to take on the enemy's main forces. Rather, it was hoped that it would be able to delay and disrupt enemy forces in the early stages of any invasion. As the chapter makes clear, the aim was to fortify men – who at best had not seen action in more than 20 years – with a confidence that, with determination and improvisation, they would be able to throw a sizeable spanner in the cogs of the enemy's war machine.

The Home Guard Training Manual (1942)

THE OBJECT OF THE HOME GUARD

1. A New Force. The Home Guard is a new kind of armed force, created because the new methods of invasion used by the Nazis cannot be dealt with only by the Army, Navy and Air Force.

The Home Guard is not a spare wheel kept in readiness to be fitted if anything goes wrong with the others. It is an essential part of the machinery with which Britain is being defended.

The Home Guard is not simply a body of veteran soldiers and civilians in reserved occupations, brought together as a last supply of reinforcements. Its duties begin at the very beginning of invasion, and it supplements the other armed forces of the Crown by doing jobs which no one else can do.

For you to understand why your services are vital, you must know something about the Nazi method of invasion. Your duty is to help destroy the smooth working of this method, and particularly to destroy the two chief advantages which the Nazis have so far had on their side, Surprise and Speed.

2. The Experience of Other Countries. The Nazis have invaded Poland, Denmark, Norway, Holland, Belgium, France. In every case the chief reason for their rapid success was that the invaded country had nothing like the Home Guard. The civilian population was not organized to resist, did not know what it could do, was taken unawares, and was terrorized by the Nazi methods.

The chief lesson we can learn from these successful invasions is that, unless the civilian population is organized to take its part in resisting the Nazis, no army or air force, or navy in the world can succeed against them.

But the laws of war, which must be obeyed by every British subject, whether or not they are obeyed by the Nazis, do not permit of civilians offering armed resistance, unless they are organized in a regular corps and wear a recognizable uniform.

That is why people, who would otherwise be civilians, have to join the Home Guard and receive uniform, in order to conform to the rules of war and at the same time to offer the necessary armed resistance to the invader.

The form which this armed resistance will take becomes clear, if we consider how the countries so far invaded met their disasters.

3. How the Nazis Invade. In Norway and Holland, for example, the Nazi method of invasion consisted of four chief parts. If when the Nazis try to invade England they adopt the same method, you must ask yourself what you and your comrades ought to do to frustrate the Nazi plans at each of the four stages.

The four chief parts of the Nazi method are as follows:

(*a*) The planting of Fifth Columnists, with instructions to help invading forces when the time comes.

Thus, in Norway, when the Nazi ships steamed up Oslo Sound, the electric mines did not go off, because Fifth Columnists had arranged to have their fuses withdrawn: the shore batteries did not open fire, because Fifth Columnists had seen to it that the order to fire should not be given. In the same way Fifth Columnists prepared the way for parachutists and transport planes to land at the airports without meeting with any resistance from the Norwegian armed forces.

(*b*) Relying upon preparations already made by Fifth Columnists, parachutists dropped on and near Stavangar airport, just as they did a little later on and near the Rotterdam airport in Holland. The duty of these parachutists was to clear away any obstacles to landing, and to prevent any resistance being organized during the fatal few minutes before.

(*c*) Transport planes landed troops at the rate of several thousand every half-hour.

(*d*) Having by these three means secured the vital places of landing by sea and air (and crossed land frontiers in the case of Holland); having also brought complete confusion to the armed forces of the victimized nation by carrying the attack into all sorts of places far behind the expected points of danger, the Nazis were able to pour in large and completely equipped forces without any fear of opposition.

Your duty is to consider how far any one of these stages in a plan for invasion might be attempted in your locality; and, from your intimate knowledge of that locality to think out methods of resistance, and to train yourself to resist them.

4. Surprise and Speed. Modern inventions have so increased **Surprise** and **Speed** that the attacking force in any war has a tremendous advantage. For the moment we are on the defensive, and therefore the advantages of **Surprise** and **Speed** are all on the Nazi side. But we must remember that we shall not always be on the defensive. Sooner or later we shall attack. Wars are won by attack, not by remaining on the defensive. When our turn comes, **Surprise** and **Speed** will lead to the destruction of our enemies.

You must realize that very often the best way of defending is to attack. Your job is not simply to prevent yourself and your village from being destroyed. At the right time you can destroy the invading enemy.

5. Surprise. We have a very long coastline; and everything that the Nazis have done on the Continent of Europe, from the successful invasion of Norway to the successful invasion of Northern France, has increased the length of our coastline opposite which they can establish naval and air bases. Their bases are now in some parts, such as the Straits of Dover, only a few minutes flying time away, and only an hour or so sea time away.

No navy or air force that can be imagined could possibly prevent invading forces successfully slipping across to our side of the water somewhere if they tried at a dozen or so different points at once.

The Nazis have already got their plans. They decided, perhaps years ago, what stretches of beach, or what harbours would serve their purpose best when the time came. They have accurate maps of hundreds of flat fields or open downland suitable for the landing of troops by transport plane. They know their plans, or more probably their alternative plans, to the last possible detail: we are in the dark.

To prevent ourselves being surprised, therefore, we must keep a watch on every inch of beach, and on every acre of land suitable for use by transport planes. Unless the Home Guard has been successfully trained to keep all these points under expert observation for twenty-four hours in the day, the Nazis can carry out at least the early stages of an invasion. There is only one way, in fact, of preventing the Nazi's **Surprise** and that is by successful, trained **Observation**.

Your first duty is to meet **Surprise** with **Observation**.

6. Speed. The Generals of the defeated armies of the Continent, including the French Generals, have entirely under-estimated the increase of Speed in military operations since the last war. We read of bridges which were not blown up, so that the Nazi tanks thundered over them. Usually this criminal negligence was due to the General Staff imagining that the Nazis could not possibly arrive until next Thursday, when in fact the Nazis did arrive on Monday.

The **Speed** of the Nazi invasion depends upon two things: first, motor or mechanized transport; second, the very skilful timing of each separate military operation, so that it can take its place exactly where it should in the general time-table of the invasion as a whole.

You must smash the Nazi timetable by reducing the **Speed** of any units of mechanised forces that happen to come your way; first, by making it difficult or impossible for armoured units to pass along the roads in the district which you are defending (this is done by skilfully prepared and staunchly held roadblocks and obstructions); second, by destroying tanks and motor vehicles.

It is a good thing to be able to hold these up, even for half an hour, because then they will be late in reaching whatever the general Nazi objective may be, and will that far upset the time-table; but it is far better to be able to destroy them, so that they never reach their objective at all.

You must know the right and the wrong way of obstructing roads, and how you and your comrades, even without any help from the military, can destroy formidable adversaries such as tanks, and cars carrying machine-guns.

7. A New Kind of War. The tasks you must carry out in co-operation with the Army and other Armed Forces are many of them quite new to British military experience. No British road or street has had to be barricaded for centuries. No British subject living in Great Britain has had to be called upon to destroy an invader in our own countryside. Moreover, our Army has not hitherto been trained for this sort of war.

This means that to be a Home Guard offers you real opportunity for adventure. We are faced with a menace. There are no answers in the older military text books. We are, in fact, in the same position as the militiamen in Republican Spain, or the Finnish soldiers in the war with Russia. We have to face an exceptionally well-equipped invader, and find out for ourselves the best way of dealing with him.

It is as well for The Home Guard to understand exactly what is meant by "guerrilla fighting."

The Home Guard will fight not as a piece moved forward in a complicated game of chess, not supported by artillery or helped by reconnaissance planes, or covered by tanks, but as isolated units either preventing the Nazis moving into their desired positions, or making life miserable and impossible for the Nazis when they are trying to occupy a piece of territory which they have temporarily overpowered. At the same time the Home Guard will always as long as possible be under the operational control of the local military commander in direct descent from the Commander-in-Chief, Home Forces.

The Home Guard preparing himself for guerrilla fighting needs therefore, quite different training. He must be even more self-reliant than any other soldier, and whereas the others must be first and foremost skilled technicians, he must be a hunting animal, relying on his own commonsense, his skill in moving and shooting, and his knowledge of the country through which he is hunting.

8. Weapons to Frighten. The weapons of modern mechanized warfare, tanks, dive-bombers, and the rest, are alike in one particular at least; their bark is worse than their bite.

A thirty-ton tank lumbering along an English country lane is a terrifying object: but it is also a helpless one. Treat it right, and it will very soon cease to be a source of danger.

Part of your training, therefore, is to study methods, many of them very strange, of putting out of action even large tanks and the most modern of automatic weapons.

9. Your Weapons. In order to carry out these tasks you must, of course, have the right weapons.

The rifle is the king of weapons, and every Home Guard must practise rifle shooting. Rifle drill is an important, though not the most important, part of his regular training. But in the new kind of warfare which he must learn there is place for all sorts of new weapons. Shot-guns may be as valuable as rifles themselves on many occasions.

Very often the conditions of fighting will be the same as when Chicago gangsters find themselves up against G-men and in these cases the weapons usual on such occasions, especially the Tommy-gun or the bomb, will be better than either a rifle or a shot-gun.

But we must not rely on these alone. Everybody knows that the British Empire is straining every nerve to increase the armament of the men defending it. But there is a great shortage to make up; and you may find yourself supplied last of all.

That does not mean that you must settle down to being poorly armed. Learn how the Spanish people used sticks of dynamite, blankets steeped in petrol, railway sleepers, a few yards of iron railing, to destroy the tanks sent against them. Learn how the Finns, because they were not wealthy enough to buy all the necessary anti-tank guns or mines for the roads, invented the "Molotov cocktails" and small home-made mines with excellent results.

You are already far better equipped than were the Spanish militiamen, who held up General Franco for many months outside Madrid; and some of you are as well-equipped as the Finns, who held up the enormous Russian armies on their frontier for more than three months.

10. Tactics. When you are learning how to use your weapons it is not sufficient to know how to load, fire, clean and strip them. Of course, you must be a good shot, because otherwise you will be useless, but having learned to shoot straight, you must learn *when* to shoot.

For example, anyone except a thoroughly experienced soldier is apt to fire too soon. It is particularly important for the Home Guard to realise the importance of holding their fire whenever this is possible. The man who knows how to get within fifty yards of his enemy unseen, and to lie up until the right moment to shoot and get away again unseen so as to shoot another day, has multiplied the number of rounds of ammunition with which he has been supplied tenfold.

It is not sufficient to know how to shoot a rifle at a rifle range. You will not be shooting Nazis on rifle ranges. You must practise shooting under very adverse conditions, for example, through smoke.

It is a very different matter to arrange oneself at one's leisure in a comfortable position so as to shoot at a target and to know how to be ready to shoot at any moment from any position, however uncomfortable, and with little or no warning.

Again, you must understand the tactical value of your weapons. A very good example of what this means is afforded by the Tommy-gun. This is an entirely new weapon to most people in the Home Guard. In consequence, you hear of people who have learned to shoot through the sights and try to shoot accurately at two hundred yards, but the Tommy-gun is not meant for this kind of shooting. The tactical use of the Tommy-gun is rather like the use of a pistol. It is for close-in fighting, where visibility is bad and you come on your enemy very suddenly. It was invented for fighting at street corners, and it is invaluable for all street fighting and in wood fighting, and also for clearing a room in a house occupied by the enemy. In these conditions you do not have time to aim through the sights, and you will therefore do much better if from the very start you get used to shooting from the hip and advancing round corners or through undergrowth with your finger on the trigger.

In the same way every weapon has its tactical use, and every Home Guard *must* be trained in the tactical use of his weapons.

11. Your Countryside. Having thus got some idea of the way in which the Nazi invasion is likely to take place, and how you can prevent it, you should take a look at your own countryside.

Most of the British countryside, especially in the most vulnerable areas, is ideal for the kind of defence which you are called upon to organize. It is exactly the sort of country which is a nightmare to the Nazi.

Compare Poland with England. Most of Poland is part of the great Central European Plain. It has few mountains and few little streams. It is easy to sweep across it in any direction at great speed. Nature does absolutely nothing to help the defenders with obstacles.

Now think of the typical English countryside – small fields, surrounded by hedges or walls or ditches, dozens of little streams, hills and valleys, numbers of woods, crooked winding roads, all the raw material for successful defence by small bodies of determined men.

In order to appreciate what a tremendous help nature offers the defenders of Britain, you must know something of the sort of tactics which can best be used in broken and enclosed country. You have heard of the Khyber Pass. Half the roads in England can be made as dangerous for an attacking force as the Khyber Pass, provided you know how to take advantage of hedges and ditches, woodland, steep gradients and sharp corners. (See Section 3).

Never forget in all your training that detailed knowledge of the countryside is the most valuable asset in the sort of war you will have to fight in a Nazi invasion – and it is the one thing you can have and the Nazi cannot have.

That is why training is a twenty-four-hour job. There is never a moment when you cannot learn something useful for resisting invasion. Get out of your mind altogether the idea that training begins and ends in the drill hall or in exercises with your unit. You can train yourself at work, in the dinner hour, in bed going to sleep, on every walk or ride through the country you have to defend.

12. Co-operation with the Army. Once you understand the sort of tactics to use against the Nazis, and once you know how to take advantage of the natural defences of your locality, you will be able to think out all the problems of local defence, which are bound to be different for every town and village in the country.

But you will not be expected to undertake the whole defence, even in your own village. You are working in co-operation with the other armed forces; and you must know how the Army is organized, what part it will take in defence, and what part it will leave to you. You must learn, therefore, what military forces there are in your locality, how to get in touch with them, how to do your job without hindering them in doing theirs. Just as you have to understand something about the various parts of a rifle, in order to use it and clean it, so you must know what the parts of an army are, and why they exist.

13. **The Lessons of Crete**. Since this Training Manual was first published, the Germans have successfully invaded Yugoslavia, Greece, Crete, and unsuccessfully invaded Russia.

Fresh lessons for us in the Home Guard can be learned from all these, but especially from the experiences of Crete and Russia.

Crete was a dress rehearsal for the invasion of Britain. The invasion had to be carried out entirely by airborne troops, because our Navy prevented sea landings. It was successful because we were unprepared to meet it in several different ways. We had not yet learned how to defend airfields, or to improvise new ones quick enough. This is not, however, a matter for the Home Guard. However, certain other deficiencies concern the Home Guard very closely.

Here is a summary of the lessons of Crete as it affects our training and duties.

German prisoners informed our Military Intelligence that our positions were given away from the air by being badly concealed, and that steel helmets particularly were extremely visible. Long before any troops were landed from planes, two other things had happened. The order of events was:–

(1) The Germans sent reconnaissance planes to photograph the whole area which they proposed to attack.

(2) Whenever they saw on their photographs signs of a defended position, they made a concentrated dive-bomber and fighter machine-gun attack.

(3) Only after everything revealed by the photographs had been bombed from the air were parachute troops dropped from planes and gliders, on and around the airfield selected for attack.

(4) After the parachute troops came airborne troops carried in planes or gliders, the parachute troops having prepared the way for them by putting the defenders out of action as far as they could, and clearing the runways for aircraft to land.

(5) Having thus got off to a good start, they supplemented their other methods of landing troops by crash-landing aeroplanes on level pieces of ground in the neighbourhood without counting the loss.

(6) Having in this way landed a formidable force from the air, all their troops united together against a common objective.

The lessons for the Home Guard include the following:–

(1) Since the enemy does not attack except after careful and detailed reconnaissance from the air, followed by dive-bombing, it is of no use when preparing defended positions and taking up action stations only to think of the enemy on the ground. Positions must be well concealed, and the enemy's reconnaissance made as confused as possible by dummy positions.

(2) The enemy did not attempt to dive-bomb special targets with individual planes. They bombed the whole of the area that they had found to be defended, so as to put anything out of action that happened to be within the area. Unless the defenders were prepared for this kind of air attack, they found it very demoralising. The lessons for the Home Guard from this fact include the following:–

(a) All your posts must be as small as possible and carefully camouflaged. The slit trench gives the best protection.

(b) Alternative positions must be sited, if possible, with a covered approach.

(c) You must not open fire on targets out of effective range, as this gives away positions without producing results.

(d) You must get accustomed to noise and not let it worry you.

(3) **Parachute attacks**. Parachute troops were dropped from about 300 feet from aircraft and gliders. Those that dropped in range of defenders were easily disposed of. They used bomb craters for immediate cover. They landed on sides of hills as well as on the flat. Arms containers had different coloured parachutes. Each man carried an automatic pistol, four hand grenades, a large knife, and a sketch map showing his job. In some cases, Tommy-guns were

strapped on to their backs. Remaining equipment (L.M.Gs. light mortars, tommy-guns, Very pistols and ammunition) was dropped in containers.

Their morale was very low unless they had time to organise after landing. When attacked at once they were easily disposed of.

Small arms fire against descending parachute troops was only effective at short range.

The lessons for the Home Guard in this include:–

(*a*) Parachute troops must be attacked at the earliest opportunity. Every second counts in making your plan and carrying it out. Every moment lost will cost you lives and ammunition. Risks must be freely taken in order to gain time. The enemy must be sought out and destroyed.

(*b*) You must not wait for parachute troops to attack you.

(*c*) Memorise covered approaches to all points in your area where they may land.

(*d*) If possible prevent them from reaching their arms containers; the weapons they carry on them are only short range, so you can snipe them while you are out of their range.

(e) Authority has been given for Home Guard sub-units to form mobile fighting patrols for this role of anti-parachutist action.

14. The Lessons of Russia. In passing, it is worthwhile noting that, in Yugoslavia, in spite of the rapidity with which the Germans put the Army out of action, they have even yet failed to occupy a very large part of the country.

Yugoslavia is an example of what can happen when a nation cannot put up a show in the "big war," but can put up a grand show in guerilla or "little war." The Yugoslav Army was not fitted in personnel, training or equipment to offer permanent resistance to the German panzer divisions and air-power, but the people of Yugoslavia, retiring to their mountains and forests, have made it impossible for the Germans to carry out the subjugation of the country.

In Russia we see what happens when a country has both got the facilities for waging big war, and the courage and spirit to continue little war.

The lesson of Russia for the Home Guard is that Armies can only oppose the German invaders if they have the active, ruthless and aggressive co-operation of the whole of the people to back them up.

The Home Guard must regard it as an essential part of their training, especially in country districts, to be able, if necessary, to live off the country, to hide up in woods, to sleep in the open and carry on in isolation while the Germans are in temporary occupation of their locality. This is as much part of their training as any knowledge of weapons, anti-tank measures or guard duties.

CHAPTER 2
ORGANISATION

The Home Guard occupied a unique position within the organisation of the forces defending the United Kingdom. They were initially a uniformed civilian militia and not part of the regular armed forces. Nor were they subject to military discipline, infractions and failure to carry out Home Guard duties punishable by the civilian authorities. The government maintained that all Home Guard duties were only to be carried out in approved uniform and that, as such, the Home Guard were lawful combatants under the Geneva Convention. A Home Guard volunteer could, however, withdraw at any time with 14 days' notice.

Much of this changed from February 1942, with the introduction of conscription for the Home Guard. Although allowed to resign before that date, all those in the Home Guard from 16 February 1942 were 'in for the duration'. From this date on the Home Guard was formally recognized as part of the armed forces of the Crown.

The Home Guard Training Manual (1942)

ORGANISATION

1. New Conditions of Service. Changing needs of the war situation have brought it about that the Home Guard which, as the L.D.V., began as a purely voluntary organisation, has had to become more strictly disciplined and with greater obligations for service.

In order to keep faith with those who had enlisted first of all on a purely voluntary basis, any member of the Home Guard was permitted to resign by February 16th, 1942. After that date, new conditions of service applied. These new conditions lay down very much more clearly the status of the Home Guard as a member of the armed forces of the Crown.

The chief changes, which should be understood by every member of the Service, can be divided into the following important subjects:

Compulsory enrollment or "conscription."
Discipline.

Training and duty.
Mustering.
Conditions relative to discharge.

A great deal of confusion and uncertainty would be saved if every man sees to it that he knows the contents of the next five paragraphs.

2. Compulsory Enrolment or "Conscription." Compulsion is now being applied throughout the country.

The reason for this is that there are certain parts where, for one reason or another, there was an insufficient enrolment in the Home Guard for the Home Guard to be able to carry locally its part in the defence plans. In most parts of Britain this was not the case.

When conscription has been imposed, it will apply to British subjects between the ages of 18 and 51, and the selection of men to be enrolled will be made by the Ministry of Labour and National Service. This Ministry will direct the selected men to report at a certain date and time to their local Home Guard unit, and will notify that unit of particulars of the men who have been so directed.

People thus ordered to join the Home Guard will have the right to claim exemption either on the grounds of conscientious objection or on medical grounds, before they are enrolled, and if, after they have been enrolled, the Home Guard Battalion Medical Officer examines them and finds them medically unfit for the Home Guard, they will be discharged at once.

If you are already in the Home Guard you need have no fear that the conscripted men will be unsuitable on grounds of security for the Home Guard, because the Ministry of Labour will consult the police on these matters before deciding to call any man up.

3. Discipline. The "housemaid's clause," whereby fourteen days' notice could be given to a Home Guard, or fourteen days' notice be given by a Home Guard, has been abolished, and from now on all members of the Home Guard are enrolled for the duration of the war or until their services are no longer required. This means that officers will no longer be able to get rid of men for breach of discipline by this method, and from now on the Home Guard will be subject to military law under certain sections of the Army Act.

There are however, some very important differences between discipline applied to a Home Guard and to a member of the Regular Army. The way in which an offence will be punished depends upon whether or not the unit to which the offender belongs has been "mustered," that is to say, ordered to proceed to action stations because an invasion has begun or is likely to begin. When, as at present, the unit is not mustered, a member of the Home Guard who, without reasonable excuse, absents himself from parade or duty will be liable on summary conviction by a Civil Court to a maximum penalty of a fine of £10 0s. 0d., or one month's imprisonment or both, that is to say, he will be summoned before a magistrate and his case will be dealt with forthwith. Before this can be done, however, authority must come from the Commander-in-Chief of the Army Command in which the unit is situated, and Command Headquarters will inform the Battalion Commander who informs the local police, who will take action.

Note that no member of the Home Guard will be ordered to do a guard duty, or any other duty, if he has a good excuse for claiming exemption from that particular duty. Full particulars of this will be found in the paragraph on Training and Duty.

Thus every safeguard has been given to members of the Home Guard. They can *(see below)* first of all make sure that they are not called upon for a duty which their civil obligations, their health or some other good reason, prevents them from carrying out. They cannot be prosecuted without their case being reviewed by a high authority. They have the right of trial in the Civil Court before a magistrate.

Directly the unit to which a member of the Home Guard belongs has been called to action stations because an invasion is expected or has begun in his locality, the situation is completely changed. He then is a serving soldier under the Army Act. He will be liable to the same punishments as a soldier for absence without leave and desertion, and for any other military crime committed while on active service.

4. Training and Duty. Quite apart from conscription, which now applies to all areas, members of the Home Guard can now be ordered to perform training and operational duty for periods not exceeding a total of forty-eight hours per four weeks. It must be clearly understood that this total of forty-eight hours is the maximum amount which can be required of any one member. The actual amount of training or operational duty to be required by his Commanding Officer of any one man will depend upon the following:–

(1) The member's civilian employment, that is to say, no Commanding Officer will demand more hours of duty than can be performed by a member of the Home Guard, bearing in mind the job he is doing in civi life.

(2) The distance he lives from the place of training. If a man has to journey several miles either from the place where he works, or the place where he lives, in order to do his Home Guard duties, this will be taken into account by his Commanding Officer when deciding how much is to be expected of him.

(3) The standard of training of the Home Guard. If, because for example, he has not hitherto turned up to sufficient instruction and drills, the

man is in a poor state of training, his Commanding Officer will order him, bearing in mind the other factors already mentioned, to come more often than better trained men to instruction and drills, so that he can make up for his slackness in the past and reach the standard of the others.

(4) The Commanding Officer will bear in mind the operational needs of the Home Guard in any particular unit that is to say, whereas for example in some large towns, there are very many men in the Home Guard, there may possibly be less need for increased hours of training and operational duties, but where as in some country districts, for example, the population is thin and the numbers small, operational duties may claim a longer number of hours per month.

The decision on all these matters will be made by the Company Commander who knows local conditions and the individual situation of the men in his Company, and he will of course receive instructions from higher authority.

It is definitely laid down in the instructions that every care must be taken to see that some men are not required to do many more hours than other men in the same unit, except when these other men are unable to perform duties for the reasons outlined above. Whenever possible, twenty-four hours a month is to be spent on actual training.

Thus the new regulations are intended to make quite certain that everybody does his share, but that nobody is unfairly treated.

5. Mustering. The Home Guard was organised strictly for local defence duties, and as a force of men living in their own homes and doing their civil jobs. It has always been perfectly clear that once an invasion has begun or is expected in the immediate future, this state of affairs may not always be possible.

The Commander-in-Chief, Home Forces, will issue the order to muster, and the order will be passed through the usual channels to Home Guard Platoons. Home Guard Platoon Commanders will be responsible for seeing that each member of their platoon is informed of the order. Once the order to muster has been given, Home Guard members will perform such a duty and at such a place as may be required of him by his Unit Commander, and there will be no maximum number of hours of service.

Certain members of the Home Guard will have to continue their civil employment as far as is possible. In the case of units recruited from men who are doing vital war work, such as factory units, railway units, public utility units and Government Department units, the managements concerned must be consulted by the Home Guard Unit Commander before issuing orders to men to leave important civil work immediately the order to muster is given.

Company Commanders are expected now to divide the men in their Company into those who are able to report for duty immediately on mustering, and those whose civil duties will have to be continued until a later stage of emergency. Each man must be warned as to whether he will be expected to report immediately for duty, and stood down later if his continued presence is no longer required, or whether he is to report to his platoon or other Headquarters for orders as soon as his civil employment permits. Even in this second case he must report within forty-eight hours, when he may be told either to continue his civil work or to proceed to action stations.

6. Conditions relative to Discharge. There is no longer any question of fourteen days' notice. All members of the Home Guard serving on 16th February, 1942, or joining after this date, will be considered to be enrolled for the duration of the war until their services are no longer required or until called up for service.

Members of the Home Guard may, however, apply for discharge for good reasons such as changed conditions of employment or residence, ill-health or hardship. The Battalion Commander will be responsible for deciding whether a discharge shall be granted. If a man is discharged from the Home Guard, he may still have to perform part-time service in the Home Guard or in some other Service, in accordance with the directions of the Ministry of Labour, subject to the usual rights of appeal.

7. Your Status as a Soldier. Apart from the matters discussed in the last six paragraphs, there are certain points about your status which you will do well to remember.

When on duty you form part of the armed forces of the Crown, and are subject to military law as a soldier.

You must obey the orders of your Commanders.

Being a member of the Home Guard does not exempt you from being called up for regular military service.

Uniforms, badges, equipment and arms issued to you are the property of the Government, not to be used except when on duty or on such occasions as your Commander orders You should remember, however, that when the invasion starts or is known to be imminent, you will be told never to part from your rifle, uniform and other equipment.

Men who work in one district and live in another will be given special orders. If you are in this position, you should ascertain now from your Platoon Commander what you are likely to be expected to do.

Your officers are holders of the King's Commission. Their usual rank is as follows:–

The Zone Commander commands an area which is usually a county or a division of counties (such as East Sussex) and has the rank of Colonel.

The Zones are divided into Battalions under a Battalion Commander with the rank of Lieut.-Colonel.

The Battalions are divided into Companies, under a Company Commander with the rank of Major or Captain.

The Companies are divided into Platoons under Platoon Commanders, with the rank of Lieutenant.

Platoons are divided into Sections, under Section Leaders wearing three chevrons (sergeant's pattern), on both arms.

Sections may be divided into Squads under Squad Leaders with one or two chevrons (corporal's pattern).

Officers of the Home Guard are in precedence junior to all regular officers of their own rank, but senior to all officers of lower rank in the Army.

8. Saluting. When the Home Guard was first formed, its Commanders did not hold the King's Commission, and it was generally considered that saluting was unnecessary or out of place.

It should be realised that there is nothing undemocratic about saluting correctly understood, and that those Armies which pride themselves upon being the most democratic of all, including the Russian Army, lay just as much stress on saluting and ceremonial discipline as the more old-fashioned Armies.

The situation has changed now that the Home Guard officers hold the King's Commission, and saluting should therefore be carried out by officers and men when they are in uniform. This does not mean that saluting should be overdone, for example, soldiers are not expected to salute every officer they meet on a crowded London street, but soldiers of the Regular Army and members of the Home Guard alike should salute the officers of both services, and saluting should always be insisted upon when a unit is on duty and orders and messages are being given and received.

9. How the Army and the Home Guard are Organised. The Army has to be organised into groups of various sizes all the way from Army Corps down to Platoons and Sections. In this way plans can be made and carried out in the most efficient manner. The officer at the head of each of these groups is responsible for carrying out certain instructions, which he in turn gets from higher officers.

Thus, because a Commanding Officer has under him a certain number of Companies, each with their Captain, he is able to trust the Captains to carry out all the details of an order as they effect the Company. Because the Captains have their Companies divided into Platoons, they are able to hand over the responsibility of carrying out certain details to the officer in command of Platoons.

In the old days at the bottom of everything was the common soldier, the ranker, who was supposed not to have to do any thinking for himself. Those days are past. The only difference between the plain soldier and any of his officers is that, although they all have to think for themselves, they have a different kind of detail to think about. This is especially true of the Home Guard.

The special type of work which the Home Guard has to carry out makes it necessary for every member of every Section to have an intelligent idea of the general plan for the defence of his locality. It is fatal for you to imagine that you can leave everything to your Company Commander, or your Platoon Commander, or anyone else. These officers are not there to save you having to think for yourself. They are there because organization helps to speed up action.

In Home Guard fighting the most important unit is the Section since poor visibility and poor communications will very often cut off the individual Section from outside advice and support. Therefore every opportunity must be taken to create good *esprit de corps* in the Section. Men in one Section should be encouraged to meet together outside their hours of duty and to compete in games and exercises with other Sections. Every effort must be made to secure Section Leaders who are trusted by their men. Every member of the Section should be trained to take the leader's place in case of a casualty.

10. Parts of the Army. The Army is divided up into different "Arms," each of which has a different task to perform, whether in attacking or defending. The chief "Arms" are as follows:

(*a*) The Infantry. Still the bulk of any army, and still having to do its fighting on foot, although nowadays infantry are usually brought to the scene of the fight in mechanised transport. Most of the regiments are by counties.

(*b*) Cavalry. These do not mean only men on horseback. In fact, there are fewer and fewer horses in the army. Soldiers fighting with mechanised vehicles such as armoured cars and motorcycles are nowadays called cavalry.

(*c*) The Royal Armoured Corps. These are the Tanks. Tanks are of different types and weights, for doing different jobs.

(*d*) The Royal Artillery. These include units of many types, all of them using guns. Among the kinds of artillery in modern war may be mentioned the Anti-Tank, the Anti-Aircraft, Coast Defence, and Searchlight Batteries.

(*e*) The Royal Corps of Signals. Modern warfare has increased the skill required in keeping up communications, and the signallers now belong to a separate arm, and consist of men with knowledge of telegraphy and wireless. There are motor cyclist despatch riders in the Corps of Signals.

(*f*)   The Royal Engineers. These are the skilled workers of the Army, and build trenches and fortifications, destroy bridges and houses, build bridges, etc.

(*g*)   The Royal Army Service Corps, which supplies food and fuel, and transports them to wherever they are wanted.

(*h*)   The Royal Army Medical Corps, with its regimental aid-posts, field ambulances, casualty clearing stations, and hospitals.

(*i*)   The Royal Army Ordnance Corps, which is responsible for all supplies except food and fuel.

Most corps are commonly called by their initials, "R. E.", for instance.

11. Yourself and other Services. In every locality the Home Guard and the Civil Defence Services must understand one another's work, and co-operate. You must acquaint yourself, therefore, with the following branches of the Civil Defence Services,

(*a*)   Air Raid Wardens. The air raid warden's duty is to help the public during an air raid, and to tell the local authority what is happening and what kind of A.R.P. services are required to deal with the situation. Air raid wardens are grouped together in the wardens' post. You should know the address of the wardens, and the wardens' posts where your Section has to operate.

(*b*)   First-Aid, or Stretcher Apparatus. These are under the control of the Local Medical Officer of Health. Their duty is to help the injured in an air raid before sending them to a first-aid post or hospital. A party consists of four men and a driver. You must know how to get hold of a first-aid party, and also the address of your local first-aid authority. There are also ambulance services, mobile units and rescue parties, and decontamination squads organised in every district.

(*c*)   The Auxiliary Fire Brigade Service. This has been organized to supplement the normal fire service, so as to deal with fires caused by air raids. You must not only know where to get in touch with these and similar services in case of emergency; you must know their personnel in your locality.

It is possible that enemy agents may pretend to be members of the Civil Defence Services in order to spread confusion and do damage in case of invasion. You must know, personally, as many people as possible, and you must satisfy yourself of the identity and good faith of any strangers who may claim to be members of Civil Defence Services. You can demand to see their identity cards if you are in any doubt.

You must not interfere with the special duties of Civil Defence workers, especially with the duties of air raid wardens during raids, although naturally opportunities will come for you to help in emergencies.

12. Police. Just as the local Home Guard gets in touch with the local military authorities when it requires military assistance, so it must get in touch with the local police authorities when it requires police assistance. The police should be informed at once of any unconfirmed reports of enemy landings by parachute or from aircraft. They must also be told of any suspicious movement of strangers or others on the roads.

13. Powers of Home Guard. Because you are a member of a part of the Armed Forces of the Crown, you are empowered by the Defence (General) Regulations, and other war-time regulations, to do things which in ordinary life you would not be permitted to do. In this you are expressly bound by law to "exercise a proper discretion"; and, if you do not exercise this discretion, you may find yourself in trouble.

On the other hand, if you do not use your powers when you should do so, you are also liable to get into trouble. You will usually be helped in making a decision by the fact that you will be given general instructions by a superior authority. The most important of your powers are as follows:

(*a*) You may arrest without a warrant. The ordinary law of the land does not permit anyone to be arrested without a written authorization signed by the proper authority, so that this power, given you for a special purpose to help you win the war, should be taken seriously. You may arrest anyone whom you have good reason to believe is likely to commit one of the following offences against the Defence Regulations:

(i) Pretending to be in government service, or a member of the police forces, or fire brigade, or auxiliary fire service. This might be done by a Fifth Column spy, or a parachutist, or even by a common thief.

(ii) Issuing false information in matters connected with the Defence of the Realm or the public safety.

You can arrest a person, in short, who is spreading false rumours, but you will certainly not do this unless you have good reason to believe that the person is deliberately spreading the rumours in order to interfere in some way with the defence of the realm.

(iii) Trying to mislead any person in carrying out their duty of helping the defence of the realm. For example, if you found a person deliberately misdirecting a military unit, and had reason to believe that the person was doing this to hinder some military action.

(iv) Interfering with telegraph, telephone, or wireless communications.

(v) Doing any act with intent to assist the enemy; e.g. signalling with lights, or obstructing a railway line, etc.

(vi) Taking unauthorized photographs of prohibited subjects, which include a very large number of scenes, military and otherwise.

(vii) Having a wireless receiver in a motor car.

(viii) Trespassing or loitering round some place of military importance, such as a factory or dock.

(ix) Failing to observe the conditions under which suspected persons are allowed to be at liberty. This means, for example, an alien who while permitted to remain at liberty, provided he reports to the police, or does not move out of a certain area or after a certain time of day, breaks these rules.

(x) Looting in war areas.

(xi) Trespassing on agricultural land, so as to injure growing crops, particularly in the case of people trampling over growing crops in order to look at a crashed aircraft or bomb crater.

(xii) Taking souvenirs from a crashed enemy aircraft.

(xiii) Endeavouring to cause disaffection, or to persuade people to evade military service, or to discourage persons from volunteering in the Forces or Civil Defence Service, or to interfere with training, discipline, or administration of these Forces.

You will see that very great tact indeed is needed, especially if a person is reported to you by a third party. Whenever possible you should take the advice of your Section Leader, or the local police. You don't want to hurt feelings or make the Home Guard ridiculous or unpopular by unnecessary action.

(*b*) You are permitted to detain persons suspected of any of these acts in custody, until you can get in touch with the police; but it must not be for more than twenty-four hours.

(*c*) You may require anyone to show you their National Registration Identity Card, and anyone who fails to produce it to you on demand must name a police station at which he will produce it within two days.

(*d*) If anyone tries to prevent you carrying out these duties, you may arrest him.

(*e*) You are not permitted to enter and search premises, unless you have been given a search warrant, signed by a Justice of the Peace, to enter particular premises to search them for evidence of an offence against Defence Regulations. In urgent cases you may be given authority to make such a search by a police officer of rank not lower than that of Superintendent. Unless you have got such authorization, you may do nothing; but, if you have it, you may also search anybody found on the premises, or whom you reasonably believe to have just left the premises. But you must not yourself search any woman.

You may seize any article, for example, a pistol, or a large-scale map, or a wireless transmission set, etc., which you believe to be evidence that the Defence Regulations have been or are about to be broken.

You may use necessary force to obtain entry into the premises, once you have been authorized to search them; i.e., you may break down a door, or force open a window.

(*f*) Anyone driving a vehicle on the road must stop, if you require him to do so, provided you are in uniform and on duty; otherwise you have no right to stop anyone, unless you have reasonable grounds for suspecting him of breaking the Defence Regulations. You may also search any vehicle standing on the public highway, or in a public place, if you have reasonable grounds for suspecting that it contains evidence that an offence is or is about to be committed against the Defence Regulations.

You may inspect any motor vehicle left unattended by the roadside, and, if it has not been locked up or made incapable of being driven, you can take steps to render it incapable of being driven; but these steps must be reasonable. You cannot injure the engine. You should not deflate all four tyres; though you may deflate one. Use commonsense in this, as in everything else.

(*g*) In the same way you can take steps to see that black out regulations are being carried out, and you can for this purpose enter premises showing a light.

(*h*) You may walk over any property without being regarded as a trespasser, if it is necessary for carrying out any of your powers under the Defence Regulations. The military may give you permission to use any land or buildings for the purpose of building obstructions or fortifications. In other words, you do not have to ask the permission of the owner of a field before you build an anti-tank obstruction across it. You may also pull down, destroy, or render useless anything placed in, on, or over land.

In carrying out all these powers you are forbidden to tell anyone secret information you may discover.

14. Pensions and Allowances. As a member of the Home Guard, and therefore a part of the armed forces, you are entitled to claim disablement allowance in respect of disabilities attributable to service in the Home Guard.

If the disability is permanent or of a prolonged nature you may be entitled to a pension award. The scale of the allowance varies according to the amount of disablement caused by the injury. These pensions are the same as if you were a private soldier, and the same rules apply to them. If you are killed on duty, your widow is entitled to a pension. A man who desires to claim disability allowance or pension should consult his company or platoon commander at the earliest opportunity.

15. Subsistence.

(*a*) When mustered for operational duties or attending courses of instruction the Home Guard will be fed under normal Army arrangements.

(*b*) When employed on duty under circumstances when feeding must be arranged by yourself, subsistence allowance is paid as follows:–

  (i.) Continuous duty of 5 hrs. but less than 8 1*s*. 6*d*.

  (ii.) Continuous duty of 8 hrs. but less than 15 3*s*. 0*d*.

  (iii.) Continuous duty of 15 hrs. but less than 24 4*s*. 6*d*.

  (iv.) Each successive period to be calculated in the same manner.

(*c*) Period of duty, as above, must be continuous.

(*d*) Period begins with reporting for duty and ends with time of ceasing duty. Time spent in travelling from residence or business is not counted.

(*e*) Claim is not valid unless extra expense on food is actually incurred.

(*f*) No claim will be made unless member concerned wishes to make one.

CHAPTER 3

ARMS DRILL

Drill was something of a contentious issue throughout the Home Guard's existence. Some units prided themselves on being as slick and smart in their drill exercises as any regular unit, while for others drill was an unnecessary anachronism and emphasis was placed almost exclusively on guard duties, patrolling and field exercises. John Brophy, author of *Home Guard Drill and Battle Drill*, from which the extract in this chapter is taken felt there was a useful middle way to be walked. Brophy was a veteran of World War I, having lied about his age and signed up aged only 14. He served in the infantry and was honourably discharged in 1918. He would go on to become a prolific author both between and after the wars. During World War II, Brophy served in the Home Guard and wrote numerous manuals on a range of subjects to supplement Home Guard training. In the foreword to the above manual, Brophy recommended that "a course should be steered between parade ground maniacs and those commanders who… are tempted to brush aside drill as unnecessary and out of date." In a civilian volunteer force where men from different social, professional and military backgrounds could find it difficult to set those differences aside, Brophy felt drill possessed certain "psychological virtues," teaching the soldier "the value of discipline and prompt obedience" as well as "self-respect and self-confidence."

Home Guard Drill and Battle Drill (1943)

ARMS DRILL

For Home Guard purposes Arms Drill means exercises with the rifle. Ceremonial uses of the rifle (except the Present Arms, a salute to officers of the rank of major or higher which affords excellent practice in the easy handling of the rifle) will not be treated here. Instruction in Arms Drill should always be combined with instruction in the care of arms, including cleaning and examination of mechanism, and practice in aiming and firing. The purpose of Arms Drill is to teach men to move with their rifles in an orderly and economical way and to handle their weapons with expert ease.

Concerning all the exercises which follow, it should be taken as read that, when marching, the disengaged arm should be allowed to swing freely, as in Squad Drill without Arms, and that when the rifle is being moved in the course of an exercise the head should be kept upright and steady unless specific instructions are given to the contrary. Most of these exercises can be performed on the march, and in that event each part of the movement is carried out as the left foot meets the ground. Arms Drill at the Halt is done at the rate of one second for each "motion" or part of a complete movement, with a slight but deliberate pause between motions.

ORDER ARMS

"SQUAD! ORDER – ARMS!"

This, or Slope Arms, is the normal position of attention when rifles are carried. It will be adopted when Falling-in, until the dressing and covering off is completed, after which the men Stand at Ease and then Stand Easy. But note that when dressing the front rank extends the *left* arm and not the right to take distance from the man on the *left*.

For Order Arms the man holds his rifle at his right side, perpendicular, the butt plate on the ground, its toe (or front) in line with the toe of his right boot. He holds the rifle with his right hand (his arm slightly bent) at or near the band, the back of his hand to the right, his fingers together and pointing downwards along the stock of the rifle, his thumb against his thigh. The trigger-guard faces the front, and forearm and rifle should be close to the body. (Diagram K)

THE ORDER
DIAGRAM K

STAND AT EASE

"SQUAD! STAND AT – EASE!"

The left foot is moved about twelve inches to the left, clear of the ground, so that both feet take the weight of the body. At the same time the upper part of the rifle is pushed forward with the right hand until the right arm is straight. The toe of the butt remains in position alongside the toe of the right boot, and the left arm by the side. This is a slightly more comfortable position than the Order Arms. It does not mean relaxation of alertness. (Diagram L)

Front view   Side view

STAND AT EASE

DIAGRAM L

STAND EASY

"SQUAD! STAND – EASY!"

The right hand is slid up the rifle to the piling swivel, and thereafter the men are free to talk.

NOTE: – *As soon as the Commander or Instructor speaks the cautionary word of command "Squad" the men should slide their hands down their rifles, thus adopting the position of Stand at Ease, and remain alert for further orders. From Stand at Ease they may be brought to the Order Arms position by the command, "Squad! Attention!"*

THE SHORT TRAIL

"SQUAD! SHORT TRAIL – ARMS!"

The rifle is held perpendicular as in the Order, but lifted about three inches clear of the ground. This movement is sometimes ordered when troops are to be moved a short distance or are ordered to take up a new position, as "At the Short Trail, etc., etc."

SLOPE ARMS (FROM THE ORDER)

"SQUAD! SLOPE – ARMS!"

This movement is performed in three motions, which are usually practised by numbers.

One. The rifle is canted or thrown upwards almost vertically at the right side. The right hand then releases its grip and catches the rifle again, this time at the small of the butt, just behind the trigger guard. At the same time, the left arm comes across the chest and close to it, in a horizontal position, and the left hand catches and steadies the rifle just below the band. The back of the left hand faces the man's front, the thumb is on the inside part of the stock, next the body, the fingers grip from the other side. The thumb of the right hand, on the small of the butt, is kept to the left, and the right arm is nearly straight. Care should be taken to throw and catch the rifle so that it is held close into the right side, and the shoulders should be square to the front. (Diagram M1)

Two. The right hand takes most of the weight and carries the rifle across the front of the body, holding it vertical most of the way, and bringing it to rest on the left shoulder. The angle and the position can be determined by these checks: the left hand grips the brass heel of the butt, wrist underneath, fingers uppermost, and in this position the left forearm and upper arm make a right-angle. The upper arm is perpendicular to the ground and the elbow close to the side so that the rifle (viewed from the front) makes a line parallel to the line between the man's nose and where his heels touch. Any tendency to move the muzzle to right or left out of this line should be corrected by moving the butt nearer or closer to the body. The right hand is retained on the small of the butt and, as soon as the rifle rests on the shoulder the fingers may be straightened. In this movement it is important to avoid any swaying of the shoulders or moving of the head. (Diagram M2)

One   Two   Three

SLOPE FROM THE ORDER

DIAGRAM M

Three. The right hand is "cut away" sharply to the side, in the normal attention position. (Diagram M3)

NOTE: – *The American rifles with which many Home Guard units are equipped are not altogether comfortable at the slope, and on the march, as apart from drill movements, it may be a good idea to carry them as American soldiers carry them, i.e. at the normal slope but with the toe of the butt pointing to the ground and the sights uppermost. The improvement in balance and comfort is astonishing.*

ORDER ARMS (FROM THE SLOPE)

"SQUAD! ORDER – ARMS!"

Three motions again.

One. With a firm grip of the left hand on the butt, pull the rifle straight down at the left side, till the left arm is fully extended. The right hand comes horizontally across the chest to steady the rifle near the band. (Diagram N1)

One   Two

ORDER FROM THE SLOPE

DIAGRAM N

Two. The right hand now takes the weight and carries the rifle across the body to the Short Trail position, i.e. vertical at the right side, butt about three inches above the ground. The only difference is that the left hand steadies it near the muzzle. (Diagram N2)

Three. The rifle is lowered, under control and without noise, and the left hand is "cut away" to the side. This is the Order Arms position. (Diagram K)

PRESENT ARMS

"SQUAD! PRESENT – ARMS!"

This movement should always be carried out from the Slope. If, through an oversight of the Commander or Instructor the command is given while the Squad is at the Order or even Standing at Ease, the Squad should, without delay or further instructions, first Slope Arms and then go through the three motions of the Present.

One. The right hand comes across and takes a firm grip on the small of the butt. The forearm is kept close to the body and horizontal. This is the same position as "Slope Arms by Numbers – Two!" (Diagram M2)

Two. The right hand, taking the weight of the rifle, lifts it clean away from the shoulder (without lowering the butt towards the ground) and holds it in a perpendicular position in front of the body, trigger-guard pointing to the left. At the same time, the left hand, with fingers and thumb extended and close together, is clapped to the stock so that the forearm lies along it, the wrist is near the magazine, and the fingers point upwards. The thumb should be in line with the mouth, and both the right elbow and the butt as near to the body as is comfortable. (Diagram O1)

Two   Three
PRESENT FROM THE SLOPE
DIAGRAM O

Three. The right hand still takes the weight and brings the rifle down, perpendicular, in front of the centre of the body, holding it about three inches away from the chest and belly, and turning the trigger-guard to the front. The right arm should be at its full extent, and the fingers of the right hand should slant downwards and be held together on the small of the butt. The left hand releases its grip and then meets the rifle again (as it slides down and is turned) at or near the band, gripping outside the sling with the thumb pointing upwards.

At the same time, the right foot is lifted slightly and placed so that the inner side comes against and behind the left heel. Once this position is achieved it will be found more comfortable and steady to let the left hand take most of the weight of the rifle and use the right hand chiefly for steadying. (Diagram O2)

INSPECTION OF ARMS

"SQUAD! FOR INSPECTION, PORT – ARMS!"

If the Squad is at the Order, each man throws his rifle up and across his body, trigger-guard to the left and downwards, and catches the rifle again with his right hand on the small of the butt and his left hand, gripping from underneath with thumb and fingers, just in front of the fore-end of the breech. Both elbows should be close to the body, the left wrist opposite the left breast, and the rifle thus held in a diagonal position just clear of the body. Immediately the safety catch should be pushed forward with the right thumb, the cut-out (if any) pulled out. The right hand man of the front rank pauses an instant to make sure all the others have released their safety catches, and the remainder draw back their bolts in time with him, glancing to the right to follow the action of his hand. As soon as the bolt is right back, each man puts his hand to the small of the butt again, thumb pointing towards the muzzle.

FOR INSPECTION PORT ARMS
DIAGRAM T

If the Squad is at the Slope when the command is given, Port Arm is performed in two motions.

One. The rifle is seized, still on the left shoulder, at the small of the butt.

Two. The right hand takes the weight and carries the rifle down and across the body to the diagonal Port Arms position, and the remainder of the movement is carried out as described above. (Diagram T)

EASE SPRINGS OR CHARGE MAGAZINES

"SQUAD! EASE – SPRINGS!"

This is done to ensure that rifles are not loaded. From the Port Arms with bolt drawn back, each man works the bolt of his rifle backwards and forwards at least five times, allowing all cartridges ejected from magazine and chamber to fall to the ground. He then closes the cut-out (if his rifle is fitted with one), pushes the bolt forward, presses the trigger, pulls back the safety-catch, and replaces his hand on the small of the butt.

"SQUAD! CHARGE – MAGAZINES!"

The American rifle holds only five rounds in the magazine. The S.M.L.E. will hold ten, but five should be regarded as the normal charge. The clip of five rounds is inserted in the breech, charger to the rear and fitting into the charger-guide. As the rounds are pressed firmly down with the right thumb, the charger is left in place: when the bolt is pushed forward it falls to the ground. The cut-out, if fitted, should be closed: otherwise the top-round should be depressed with the fingers of the left hand before the bolt is slid home, to prevent it entering the chamber. After that the trigger may be safely pressed, to relieve pressure on the springs, and the safety catch applied: or commanders may think it wiser to forbid the pressing of triggers while magazines are loaded.

CHAPTER 4
FIELD EXERCISES

Perhaps the greatest weakness of the Home Guard from its inception – shortages of uniforms, weapons and basic equipment aside – was a total lack of any relevant tactical experience. The doctrine and tactics of the BEF had been shown to be woefully inadequate during the German invasion of France, ultimately leaving British forces with their backs to the sea at Dunkirk. The military experience of veterans in the Home Guard was likely to be of the trench warfare of the Western Front during World War I and so even more outdated. British forces were learning to counter an entirely new style of warfare and while the regular army had some opportunity to develop new doctrine and tactics from experience in the Western Desert, the same was not true for Home Guard units. Field exercises were a vital method of providing Home Guard formations with tactical experience. They also helped develop the initiative and leadership amongst all ranks vital if the Home Guard was to be successful in the sort of small-unit actions that would typify their role in countering any invasion.

Advanced Training for the Home Guard (1941)

FIELD EXERCISES

Next to instruction and practice in the use of weapons, field exercises form the most important part of Home Guard training. This applies to town and city units as much as to those with stretches of open country to defend. The term "field exercise" should be taken to mean any mimic operation of war involving the use of a substantial proportion of a platoon, whether it is conducted over moors, meadows, woods and hill-sides, or in built-up areas.

The field exercise can be made to serve several valuable purposes. It should give Home Guardsmen practice in what are likely to be their duties if and when the Germans are able to make war by land in this country; it should enable them to test unpredictably, spontaneously and in circumstances continually changing, all the otherwise uncoordinated details of soldiering they have been taught. Thus a series of field exercises offers opportunities for more or less realistic practice in the use of the various Home Guard weapons, in fire control, range finding, correct aim and trigger pressure (under conditions very different from the rifle range), as well as in camouflage, taking cover, accurate observation and report, movement under fire, sniping and ambushes.

The limitations of the field exercise are obvious. It cannot reproduce the noise, the nerve strain, the casualties and the confusion of actual battle. But within these limits it should be made as realistic as possible.

SPECIMEN FIELD EXERCISES

Field Exercise No. 1.

CLEARING A SMALL WOOD OF ENEMY ON FOOT

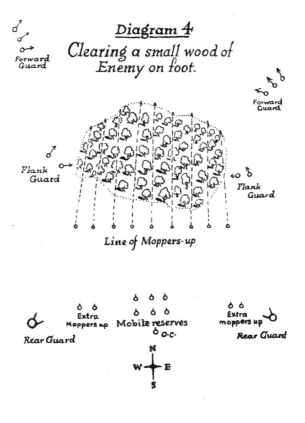

Diagram 4
Clearing a small wood of Enemy on foot.

Forward Guard

Forward Guard

Flank Guard

Flank Guard

Line of Moppers-up

Extra Moppers up

Mobile reserves
o.c.

Extra moppers up

Rear Guard

Rear Guard

N
W — E
S

On no account should the wood be entered from all sides; otherwise men are almost certain to fire on their own comrades, and amid the confusion and recriminations some of the enemy may escape. The most satisfactory method is to make a drive through the wood with a line of moppers-up. A V formation, covering the whole spread of the wood, is sometimes prescribed, but experiment has shown it to be impracticable, for the Home Guard at least. Alignment is difficult to maintain, and where there is thick undergrowth even the general direction may be lost. A single line for a straight drive through seems a better proposition. The commander should take post with a small mobile reserve and, on either side of him (but also behind the main line), small parties of moppers-up to carry out a final search.

While the wood should not, and usually cannot, be surrounded, each side of it should be covered by fire. To prevent escapes to right or left two flank guards should be posted, one on each side with orders to fire on any enemy who emerge – but not until they emerge and have been identified. Similarly two forward guards should be posted on the far side of the wood, each some twenty or thirty yards wider than the flank guard. They will fire – with similar orders – on any enemy driven out of the wood by the moppers-up.

As soon as the outside flank men of the moppers-up come abreast of the flank guards, these guards will cease to fire in such a direction that their bullets would enter the wood and endanger the moppers-up – unless at point-blank range. When this point is reached the left flank guard will change direction half left, i.e. across the further end of the wood, but taking care to avoid the forward guard. The right flank guard will similarly change the direction of its fire half right.

The moppers-up form in a straight line and preserve this alignment during their advance through the wood in order that any enemy groups encountered may be put out of action or driven out to where the flank and forward guards can fire on them.

Behind this line of moppers-up proceed the mobile reserves – with whom the operational commander might well place himself. Their task is to move swiftly towards any centre of determined resistance and put an end to it. On either side of the reserves should be placed small parties of extra moppers-up.

Two small rear-guards are left behind, one on each flank, to deal with any enemy who escape the sweep of the moppers-up and mobile reserves.

The moppers-up should proceed cautiously and quietly, disclosing themselves as little as possible and taking cover. They should search any pits, thickets, ditches and other suitable places in which the enemy may hide. From time to time they will halt to preserve formation. Inside the wood the enemy has a distinct advantage. He will have chosen firing positions in cover, and may well be able to inflict casualties before he is forced to retreat or surrender. To minimise these casualties the moppers-up should show themselves as little as possible, and move swiftly from one point of concealment to the next. They should be warned beforehand that each man is to halt, as he reaches the further margin of the wood, so as not to cross the field of fire of the flank and forward guards.

The most suitable arms for this operation are rifles with fixed bayonets and tommy guns (submachine-guns). The mobile reserve should carry in addition light machine-guns and hand grenades. The grenades should be used only under the commanders' orders, to dig out the enemy from a pit or watercourse: and it should be borne in mind that fragments of grenade casing may carry as far as a hundred yards.

The task of clearing a wood should not be undertaken except in daylight or very strong moonlight. During hours of darkness, posts should be established round the wood, roughly in the positions indicated for forward, flank and rear-guards, with order to fire only at short range and at identified enemies. The clearing operation should commence as soon as the light is suitable.

Field Exercise No. 3.

ATTACK ON A FARM

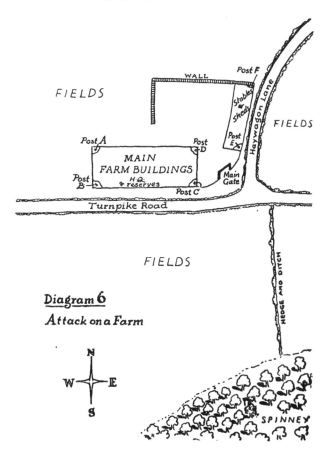

Diagram 6
Attack on a Farm

A Home Guard unit, in preparing its plans to repel invaders, will not normally expect to undertake the defence of a farm, unless it is used as a Home Guard headquarters. The great danger is that farm buildings are easily set on fire. If an enemy body, not in overwhelming force, is making in the direction of the farm (perhaps at dusk and after being roughly handled by other British troops) it may well be tempted to seize the farm and hold it as a fortified position; in such circumstances it would probably pay the Home Guard to let the enemy take possession and then make them sorry they ever allowed such an idea to enter their heads.

The diagram approximates closely to an actual farm, and field exercises have shown that there is no substantial increase of fire power to be effected by putting outposts into the surrounding fields, while the men holding them invariably are unable to retire on the main position without suffering casualties. The enemy, being strangers, may not realise this, and the first stage of any attack therefore should be to reconnoitre and then to overpower or cut off any outposts he may have established.

At zero hour the commander of the attacking force should be informed of where the enemy was last seen, and when and in what direction he was moving. He should also be given an estimate (which may later prove erroneous) of the enemy's arms and equipment. His first task is to discover if the enemy is in occupation and to deal with any outposts.

The wall round the farmyard is a hindrance to the defence; it may enable the attackers to come in close under its protection. The north-south stretch of the wall can be covered from the main building (Post A) but to bring fire to bear on anyone approaching the east-west stretch, the enemy (defence) commander must establish a post at the northern end of the stables and sheds. If he puts it at the north-east corner (Post F) it can also fire down Haywagon Lane. Post E, at the south-east corner of the stables, commands the main gate and to some extent Turnpike Road. Posts E and F should therefore be regarded as constituting an independent garrison under a subordinate commander. It is not likely they will be able to rejoin the main body of the defence if the attack gets to close quarters, and if any satisfactory strong point in the farmyard can be improvised for them to fall back upon, so much the better. On the other hand, if the attackers force a way past them to close in on the main building, they should seize their opportunity to counter attack in the rear or flank with short-range weapons.

The main farm building is defended by posts A, B, C and D, each at a corner to give the maximum width to the field of fire. Machine-guns and rifles will be placed on the ground floor (except on Post D, where it is necessary to overlook the wall); grenade throwers, etc., on the first floor and the roof. H.Q. and reserves should be in a central position.

Despite the handicaps indicated above, this is a strong position, and heavy casualties may be inflicted by the defence, with its command of the country around, at ranges from eight hundred to two hundred yards. The greatest danger to the defending army is from the incendiary weapons.

The commander of the attacking force should therefore aim at setting the main building and stables on fire. A "token" conflagration will do perfectly well for the purposes of a field exercise. If he has long-range weapons at his disposal capable of doing this, his task is simplified. The fire will drive the enemy out. (The umpires with the enemy must decide when the building is no longer habitable.) The attackers can then take prisoners as they emerge or shoot down the enemy if he tries to fight his way out. For this purpose posts must be established all round to close in as the fire spreads.

If the attack commander possesses only short-range weapons capable of setting the buildings on fire, he must find some means of getting a small party of his men to close quarters. The diagram shows that the farm commands most of the surrounding country, and there are only two feasible approaches for the incendiary party. They may come (preferably in motor transport) down Haywagon Lane and turn at speed along Turnpike Road, or reverse this approach. This must be done swiftly and the inflammable agents hurled as they go past: a hazardous and uncertain operation.

The other alternative is for the incendiary party to creep and crawl down the hedged ditch from the south or under cover of the roadside hedges. When they get to close quarters they should be covered for their final dash by fire from as many machine-guns as can be brought up, either mobile on the road or firing from the spinney. To time and direct such machine-gun fire, however, is not easy. Practice and co-ordination by signal system is needed.

This exercise should be tried first in daylight, and if the attack proves too difficult, it should be tried again by night, and a note made that in real warfare any enemy in possession should be contained there until nightfall.

Unless the local strength is exceptionally high, not more than two sections should be allotted to the defence. The attacking strength should be at least equal, except by night. Both defence and attack should be equipped with heavy and light machine-guns, tommy guns, rifles and bayonets, hand grenades and incendiary weapons.

The exercise can profitably be repeated several times, attack and defence interchanging, and the attack varying its route and methods, until every reasonable probability has been well tested.

Field Exercise No. 4.

HOLDING A FORTIFIED STREET AGAINST ENEMY WITH TRANSPORT

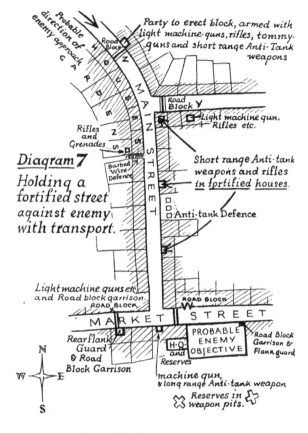

This exercise is especially suitable for urban areas, but may easily be adapted for a village. If possible, a street lined continuously with houses, neither detached nor semi-detached, should be chosen as the site for action. It is virtually impossible to pin an enemy and effect a victory in a street where gaps between houses afford ways of escape, unless the defence possesses sufficient materials, men and weapons to fortify and cover all these gaps.

In the diagram it will be seen that Main Street (where the defence commander intends to bring the enemy to action) includes a side turning to the east at the northern end, a vacant building lot on the eastern side, and a passage on the western side. These must be adequately stopped, with a road block, anti-tank obstacles and barbed wire respectively, and garrisoned.

The enemy is reported to be approaching from the north in vehicles, probably three tanks, with motor-cyclists in front, and lorry-borne infantry behind or in front of the last tank. The defence commander has already noted the large building on the south side of Market Street as a probable objective, which the enemy may try to seize and hold as part of the process of infiltrating into the town or village and capturing it piecemeal. Having prepared defences and fortified houses beforehand, and reckoning the forces and weapons at his disposal adequate to the task of giving battle to this comparatively small enemy body, he resolves to fight before the enemy reaches his probable objective at all.

The means he adopts is a variation of the tank trap in a defile; he has to reckon also with the motor-cyclist outriders and the accompanying infantry in lorries.

In choosing a Headquarters for the action and posts of his reserves, he may elect to place them nearer the junction of Main Street with Market Street. The position shown in the diagram gives him a less than perfect view, but on the other hand it provides a line of communication via houses and gardens on the east side of Main Street, which should be relatively free from fire: along this line he can send and receive messages and despatch reinforcements from his reserves. He guards his rear with two weapon pits and a rear flank guard is posted in a house on the south side of Market Street, also covering road block X.

The erection of the road blocks W and X is completed, and they are reinforced with lorries and any heavy material that may be available as soon as the report of the enemy's probable approach is received. These blocks are sited just round the corner from the southern end of Main Street, so that the enemy column sees them very suddenly and unexpectedly. The main point is that a stretch of enclosed road sufficiently long to contain the enemy transport should be blocked in all directions and so transformed into a defile.

At the appropriate time the rear road block Y in the side street and road block Z at the northern end of Main Street are erected and reinforced, and the defence garrisons take up their various posts and conceal themselves from sight. The materials for these road blocks Y and Z are left at the side of the road and made inconspicuous *until the enemy column has been halted or slowed down.*

In the diagram only two of the defence posts are shown on the west side of Main Street. A small party guards the passage between houses; another party with a light machine-gun is placed in a garden at the back of the houses at the south-western end of Main Street to fire on any enemy who may attempt to escape through houses and across gardens. Normally it is better to post riflemen on the left of a street so that they can fire from cover, but here the side turning and the vacant lot are on the right, so most of the posts are grouped there. A heavy machine-gun post is established in a fortified house on Market Street, from which it can command the length of Main Street to just beyond the bend. This should be able to put infantry dislodged from tanks or lorries, and also motor-cyclists, out of action. Close range anti-tank weapons may also be used from houses here against the forward enemy vehicles.

The advantage of placing all the other defence posts on the east side of Main Street is that they are less likely to inflict casualties on each other. The men should be warned, however, not to venture into the street, down which the heavy machine-gun will be firing. If the enemy suffers severe casualties and becomes disorganised, the men in these defence posts may, at a later stage, come into the street to finish the action, but only after ordering the machine-gun to cease firing by prearranged signal.

The general plan of the action, then, as the defence commander designs it, is that the garrisons remain concealed and do not open fire until the head of the enemy column, probably motor-cyclists, pulls up in front of blocks W and X. The concealed garrisons of the most northerly posts then quickly erect road blocks Y and Z, covered by fire from other men on these posts. Even if the chances of battle do not allow them to erect these rear blocks, they should be able to prevent the enemy withdrawing. The enemy is thus halted and, unable to turn and escape, must give battle.

The aim of the defence should be to fall on him instantaneously from a number of positions, using machine-guns, light or heavy, tommy guns, rifles, flame throwers and other anti-tank weapons. Generally speaking, anti-tank and other grenades, Molotoffs and such will be thrown from upper windows at tanks and lorries, and S.A. will be fired from ground floor windows. If anti-tank mines or explosives are used, the detonating party must be given clear space to work in.

A company is the most suitable unit to carry out this defence, or three platoons with the other platoon taking the part of the mechanised enemy, whose arms may be augmented for this occasion.

The umpires may judge that a certain number of the enemy would escape this first simultaneous assault and take up positions in the houses on the west side of Main Street. The exercise may then enter on a second stage of house-to-house fighting. This will be useful practice, but the results are difficult to judge. If possible, one umpire should be stationed at each road block and street defence post, and at least three should be with the enemy, to estimate the effect of the attack.

Field Exercise No. 5.

DEFENCE OF A BRIDGE OVER A RIVER OR CANAL

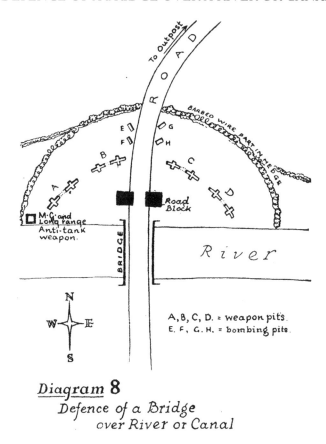

Diagram 8
Defence of a Bridge
over River or Canal

The strength of the garrison will depend on the importance of the road and the bridge carrying it across water. The road-blocks at each end will be of concrete or some other permanent material. Better results will be obtained if strong points are *not* embodied in them or sited just beside or in rear of them. This is because the garrison will probably find its view along the road obstructed, and the obviousness of the defence position may lead to the enemy concentrating high-explosives on it with disastrous effect.

In the diagram only one approach, with the appropriate defence system, is indicated, but it should not be assumed that because the enemy approaches from the north he will not also appear from the south. Even if he has crossed the river at another point, it will still be of the utmost value to deny him the use of the bridge – and relief may come speedily.

For this exercise the defence commander should not be informed of the enemy's strength or location, but left to obtain information from his outposts, which should be in visual communication with the bridge defence H.Q. and have a pre-arranged and simple system of signals.

Informed in this way of the enemy approach, the commander will man his posts, send off a message to the appropriate quarter that he expects an attack, and complete his road-blocks.

We assume that the enemy attack comes from the north. It will be met with S.A. fire from the weapon pits (each with an alternative position connected by a crawl trench) A, B. C and D. These are designed to cover the full arc of *180* degrees in which the enemy can approach the bridge and its block. He can be fired at both on the road and on the flanks if he attempts to develop an attack there.

Four bombing pits, E. F. G. and H are dug close to the roadside, and from these enemy vehicles halted or slowing up can be attacked with close-range anti-tank weapons. In addition to this, from the point X near the river bank and on a flank, long-range anti-tank weapons can be used on the enemy vehicles, and a machine-gun or other anti-personnel weapon used against the dislodged tank crews or follow-up infantry. The siting of the barbed-wire entanglement presents a problem. It must be between thirty and a hundred yards in front of the weapon pits and bombing pits, which otherwise would be exposed to attack by hand-grenades. It must not be put across the road for fear the enemy is halted too soon. This means (*a*) the road gap in the wire must be covered with heavy fire to prevent an infantry attack; *(b)* the defence commander must use every resource to halt the enemy follow-up infantry outside the wire.

As a preliminary to this engagement, the defence may be allowed to put out outposts and road-ambush parties, to obstruct and delay the enemy approach. All S.A. weapons and tommy guns should be used by the defence. The barbed wire entanglement should be concealed in a hedge or in some other way: otherwise it loses half its effectiveness. The enemy should represent a panzer section of three tanks, with motor-cyclist outriders and lorry-borne infantry in the rear.

Field Exercise No. 6.

DEFENCE OF A FACTORY

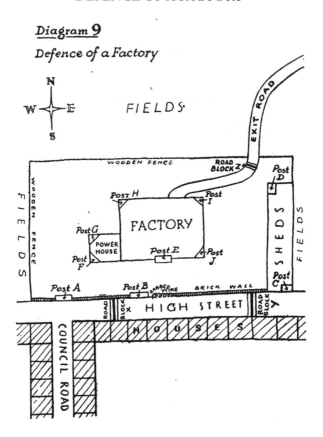

[*Note*: – In certain areas a factory Home Guard may be required to participate in the general defence scheme. It may then have to defend its premises by taking station a *mile* or more away. In general, factories will continue to work even in the event of invasion, and the Home Guard duties will be principally observation and anti-sabotage. If and when the enemy draws near, the factory Home Guard will cease production and function as part of the local defence scheme. Nevertheless, defence schemes are subject to alteration, and such exercises as this should not be overlooked.]

It is doubly important to hold a factory or works against the enemy; first to deny him occupation for either use or sabotage, and second to prevent him using the building as a temporary fortification and shelter to further his occupation of the whole town by infiltration.

The factory shown in the diagram has a fairly typical lay-out in that it faces a busy street and built-up area, is surrounded by its own fenced-in yards, and backs on to fields. The defence of factories which are closely hemmed in by other buildings involves the fortification and garrisoning of some of these buildings, patrols in vehicles or on foot, and, from the first, close-quarter fighting with such short-range weapons as the tommy gun, the hand grenade and the rifle and bayonet. It can only to a limited extent be planned in advance, and training should proceed along the lines indicated.

In order to hold successfully a factory such as that shown in the diagram the defence commander must first realise that he is liable to be attacked from any side or from all sides at once: this includes air attack. So far as possible, then, he must site his posts to give each a field of fire on two or three sides.

He will doubtless consider the establishment of outposts in the fields outside the factory premises, but it is unlikely that he would be able to dig communication trenches across the factory yard to afford the outposts a fair chance of retiring under pressure. If he can do this, all the better. Otherwise he must make up his mind to resist enemy attacks from all sides mainly by fire from posts in the factory building, power-house and sheds.

The wooden fence running round the yard presents a problem; it affords an approaching enemy cover from observation and enables him to get to comparatively close quarters. On the other hand, it would yield little protection against fire to any posts he might establish there. The defence commander has two alternatives. He can make loopholes in the fence (which we assume to be at least six feet high), and erect sandbag-walls behind them in suitable places. From these posts (not shown in the diagram) he can cover the fields to the north and west, and give the garrisons orders to withdraw to the factory and power-house if the enemy gets within a certain range. The disadvantages are that he must deplete his central garrison to man these posts, and, once they are abandoned under pressure, he yields to the enemy not merely cover from observation (the fence), but protection from fire (the sandbag walls). His other alternative is to level the fence as soon as approach of the enemy is reported. This means at least that he can sweep two sides of his position with heavy and light machine-gun fire. It has also the considerable advantage that the defence commander can station the men in Posts G, H and I, and part at least of the men in Post F, where they ought to be, i.e., on the ground floor and not higher, as they must be if they have to fire over the fence.

To hold up and repel an attack from Council Road and High Street he establishes two strong road blocks (X and Y). Post A, equipped with a bombing platform, sandbag reinforcements and loopholes in the brick wall, commands Council Road with its S.A. fire, and can also lob anti-tank bombs, and possibly grenades, on the enemy held up by road block X. Post B is the second garrison for this road block; it should be equipped also with tommy guns in case the enemy forces the block or outflanks it through the houses on the south side of High Street. If the defence commander can spare the men, he might also reinforce one of these houses and garrison it.

The main gate is commanded from Post E, and subject to flank attack also from Post B. A block, or at least a substantial barbed-wire entanglement should be erected at the gate. The most likely site for H.Q., with the reserves, is on a floor above Post E. It should afford the defence commander good all-round observation and easy means of communication within the building.

The approach from the east along High Street is guarded by road block Y, with Post C (in or on the sheds) to cover it. This is a two-sided post, and so is Post D, at the north-west end of the sheds, which covers Road Block Z and the fields to the north and east, as well as Exit Road. The men for posts C and D should be carefully chosen; they must not leave their stations if the attack develops away from them, to the north-west or the south-west; while if they are themselves heavily attacked, they are unlikely to be able to fall back on the main building.

The factory and the important power house are guarded by five posts (F. G. H. I and J), each commanding two sides, as well as by Post E facing the main gate. The siting, arrangements and use of these posts should follow the principles of riflemen and machine-gunners on the ground floor and/or first floor, observers under or on the roof, and the supplies in the cellars. The walls alone should not be relied on to give protection from fire; muzzles should not project from loopholes; and rooms should be darkened.

For the adequate defence of a factory of any size, at least two platoons are necessary. The enemy should be of approximately the same strength or even more. The exercise will be more valuable if the enemy is given transport and, after the initial stage of the attack, splits into two or more parties, attacking from several sides simultaneously.

Field Exercise No. 7.

ATTACK ON AIRBORNE TROOPS

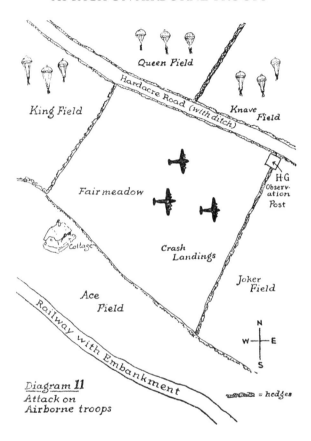

Diagram **11**
Attack on
Airborne troops

A large and fairly flat field (Fairmeadow in the diagram) is chosen by the enemy, who set out to seize it and use it as an airfield for fighter planes. Their method is to drop parachutists in three adjoining fields (King, Queen and Knave Fields), and five minutes later three troop-carrying planes are crash-landed in Fairmeadow itself. The parachutists gather their arms together and proceed to establish defence posts round Fairmeadow to the north and east, i.e. to cut off and hold Fairmeadow. The enemy disembarking from the troop carriers drag these planes to the edge of Fairmeadow, while some of them hasten to set up defence posts at the south-east corner and to sabotage the railway.

In view of the fact that Nazi parachutists may use uniform difficult to distinguish from our own, enemy troops for this exercise should not carry a distinguishing mark, and the troop-carrying planes can be represented by farm wagons or cars.

At zero hour the Home Guard commander receives a message from his observation post, by telephone, that enemy planes are flying low overhead. Five minutes later a cyclist from the post tells him that parachutists are landing in Queen Field. The three men left on the post will make it their first duty to observe and report; they will open fire only if by doing so they can inflict casualties or delay the enemy's activities without serious risk to themselves. That is all the initial information the commander should receive, and he must transmit it at once to the appropriate quarters.

He cannot denude his other posts, so he sends his second-in-command, with all the reserves he can spare, armed with heavy and light machine-guns, rifles, and perhaps a mortar to tackle the problem as it presents itself. The operation is then in the hands of the second-in-command, who arrives with his reserves on the scene of action, and is informed by the observation post that more parachutists have landed in King Field and Knave Field, and three troop-carriers have crash-landed in Fairmeadow. The second-in-command, observing the enemy activities himself, gets an idea of their general intention. He sees that all this is passed on immediately to his H.Q. with an outline of his own plan.

While he is sending this message, he orders a heavy and a light machine-gun to open fire from the point nearest to the north-east corner of Fairmeadow, on the troop-carriers and their late occupants, and also on the parachutists in Knave Field. With those in King Field and Queen Field he cannot deal there and then. He also puts out riflemen as flank and rear-guards. Despite all this, he may well be driven east along Hardacre Road.

He then perceives that the south-east of Fairmeadow is guarded by an enemy post. He decides whether he can send a patrol to stalk this post along the hedges or whether it will be quicker and more effective to send them round by road and find a place where they can come up from the east along the railway embankment. Whatever he decides to do, he includes in a message to his H.Q., and also suggests that reinforcements may be able to approach most satisfactorily by railway, but warns them to beware of sabotage on the line.

A little later the second-in-command may have been driven back some distance from Fairmeadow, but he will know that he is inflicting casualties and spreading the enemy's defences. After a time, he should be sent a message that reinforcements from the Regular Army are coming through by road, and that an increase of fire from the railway will mean that either the Railway Home Guard unit or rail-borne troops are coming into action here. If sufficient numbers are not available to give substance to this change in the situation, the umpire should effect it by informing the enemy commander. The second-in-command and his detached section (sent by hedge or road towards the railway) should then be able to advance again.

The defence commander's object is to observe and report, then to delay and harass: only when adequate reinforcements come up can he enlarge this to an attack. And his attacks (in co-operation with the reinforcements) should be planned to mop up the enemy dispositions, not all at once, but part by part. The principles of this operation are: *(a)* the Home Guard must not bite off more than it can chew or try to operate on too wide a front: it should be prepared to retire, inflicting casualties, until reinforcements arrive; *(b)* it should work from one or two sides only of an enemy landing; a surrounding operation is only likely to weaken its effort; *(c)* when reinforced, it should attack the enemy, necessarily dispersed, one part after another. In the exercise based on this diagram, for example, the concluding stages of the operation would be the mopping-up of the posts established by the troop-carrier enemy, and then of the parachutists landed in Queen Field and King Field, who should be left till then to guard flanks which will not be attacked in the first stages. Some of these may take refuge for a last stand in the cottage at the south-west corner of Fairmeadow.

Two sections can be set against two sections for this exercise, but if others are available later to reinforce the defence, the enemy strength can be increased to a platoon or more. Some anti-tank weapons may be carried in case the troop-carriers claim to have landed light tanks. The parachutists should be armed with tommy guns and grenades, and unless they take over quickly they may be put out of action by the Home Guard, operating from a greater range than tommy guns will carry, before they can get their heavier guns into action. The umpires should take careful note of the times at which the initial stages of the operation begin, and in subsequent practice every effort should be made to open fire at the earliest possible moment. For this, not only quick and accurate reporting is needed, but immediate decisions by the commander on the spot.

[*Note:* – For this exercise it is assumed that regular troops, probably with armoured fighting vehicles, are at hand, Home Guard commanders in country districts where such reinforcements are not immediately available would do well to form a Company Reserve, motorised, as a striking force against parachutists. If they obtain authority to armour-plate one or two cars, these may fight from the road-side or on occasion enter fields to crush machine-gun posts established by parachutists.]

CHAPTER 5
RIFLES AND RIFLE SHOOTING

The presence within the Home Guard of a number of veterans of the First World War created problems for the government in the early days of its formation. Many felt that they were ready to be issued weapons without requiring further training. The government's apparent reluctance to issue weapons led to impatience and bad feeling. It is worth noting, however, that alongside veteran volunteers were many men who had no military experience and there was an expectation that they would rapidly be trained to a competent standard of rifle shooting. This chapter consists of an article that appeared in *The Home Guard Training Manual* by Jocelyn Barlow who was a British sports shooter. Barlow had won a number of shooting awards before the war and competed in the 1948 and 1952 Summer Olympics after the war. He had privately published *The Elements of Rifle Shooting* before the war and continued to write articles and training manuals during the war. These are typical of the numerous private publications that supplemented official War Department materials and proved invaluable, often being subsequently adopted into official publications.

The Home Guard Training Manual (1942)

RIFLES AND RIFLE SHOOTING

By Lt.-Col. J.A. Barlow, W. York. Regt

You, as one of the Home Guard, may be armed with any one of the following rifles:

(*a*) The .303″ British Service rifle (S.M.L.E.).

(*b*) The .303″ pattern Dec. 14 rifle (P.14).

(*c*) The .303″ Canadian Ross rifle (Ross).

(*d*) The .300″ U.S.A. 1917 model which looks almost exactly like the British P.14, having been copied from it (Model 17).

(*e*) The .300″ U.S.A. Springfield rifle (Springfield).

When you first joined up you probably had a British rifle given you. If you have not already had it changed for one of the U.S.A. types, it is probable that this will happen shortly. The reason is that at first you had to be armed at once with what was immediately ready; now that large stocks of U.S.A. weapons are arriving, it is obviously better for all the Home Guard to have American weapons while the field army, which has to move about, keeps to the British types.

All U.S.A. rifles, and in fact any weapons which will not take the British Service cartridges, are marked with a red band two inches wide, in order to distinguish them. If this gets worn off, paint some more on yourself on the same spot. Use a quick drying paint.

1. Ammunition. British cartridges are issued in black steel chargers which hold five rounds. The cartridge has a rim at the base. The ordinary ball ammunition has a ring of purple lacquer round the cap, while in the case of tracer the lacquer is red. U.S.A. ammunition is rimless and is issued in small brass clips also holding five rounds.

Always clean ammunition and chargers issued to you at the first opportunity. Thereafter look the ammunition over closely and see that it is clean. Your life may depend upon it. Dirty ammunition causes slow loading.

2. To Load

(*a*) Put off the safety catch, which, on the above rifles will be found as follows:

    (i) S.M.L.E. on left at back of bolt.

    (ii) P. 14 on right at back of bolt.

    (iii) Ross, on right on bolt lever. Positions marked "READY and SAFE."

    (iv) Model 17. As on P.14.

    (v) Springfield. On back of bolt (cocking piece). The safety catch swings over sideways. Left is "READY," right is "SAFE."

(*b*) Open the bolt by raising the bolt lever and pulling to the rear – types (*a*), (*b*), (*d*), and (*e*) – or pulling straight to the rear in the case of the Ross.

(*c*) All the above rifles have charger (or clip) guides into which the charger (clip) fits. Place a charger (clip) in this "end on"; either way up. Put your right thumb on the back end of the top cartridge, curling your forefinger under the woodwork by the magazine, and force the cartridges out of the charger (clip) into the magazine.

    (i) *N.B.* In most of the S.M.L.E. rifles there is what is known as a "cut-off" on the right of the body. This, when pushed in, prevents the magazine being loaded, or, if loaded, from being used. Before charging the magazine make sure that it is pushed out to the right.

(ii) On both the Ross and Springfield rifles there is also a "cut-off" but of a different kind. This is a thumb-piece on the, left of the body. It works in three positions. When the thumb-piece points upwards, the magazine can be used, while when turned down the bolt is prevented from coming right back and so no round is fed into the chamber by the bolt. (This "cut-off" in the "down" position is of little use and should be neglected. It is of no help when magazines only have to be charged.) In the middle position, a clearance on the inside of the thumb-piece allows the bolt to be taken out of the rifle for cleaning.

(iii) Having charged the magazine, (S.M.L.E. holds ten, the P.14, Ross, Model 17 and Springfield only five rounds) push the bolt forward and down to the right or straight forward in the case of the Ross.

The rifle is now loaded.

(iv) Apply the safety catch, by reversing what you did before.

3. Points to note when Loading or Dealing with Loaded Rifles

(*a*) Never point a loaded rifle at anybody or in any direction in which harm might be done if it fired. Obviously you must use the same caution when loading.

(*b*) Never handle dummies and live ammunition at the same time. Always keep them separate.

(*c*) Always inspect both your own and other people's dummies and weapons before practising.

(*d*) If the magazine only is to be charged, leaving no round in the chamber, proceed as follows:

(i) With the S.M.L.E. use the "cut-off" if you have one, i.e. shut it before you close the bolt.

(ii) With all other rifles (including the Ross) press the top round in the magazine down with your left thumb and edge the bolt over it with your right hand, so ensuring that no round is fed into the chamber.

Having charged the magazine, snap the trigger and apply the safety catch. If you have a cut-off, pull this out again now, so that when you want to load, all you have to do is to open and close the bolt.

Warning regarding the Ross rifle bolt. It is possible to assemble the Ross rifle bolt wrongly, and to insert it into the rifle in that state. If the rifle is then fired, the bolt will be blown to the rear and the firer will be seriously injured. **Therefore, whenever you pick up your Ross make sure that the bolt is correctly assembled. Somebody may have tampered with the rifle and put the bolt together wrongly**.

How to tell if the bolt is correctly assembled. Open the breech but do not take the bolt out of the rifle. Look at the bolt-head and note its position in relation to the front end of the sleeve. The bolt-head is the extreme front part of the bolt and is distinguished by the interrupted threads on its sides, while the sleeve is that part of the bolt which covers most of the mechanism and bears the bolt-lever at the rear end. **The bolt is correctly assembled if the bolt-head is nearly one inch from the front end of the sleeve when the breech is open.**

The bolt is **wrongly** assembled if the distance between the same two parts is about **one quarter of an inch or less.**

Never attempt to fire a rifle in this condition.

4. Hints on Shooting. In order to get a shot to hit the mark, you must do three things efficiently, viz:

(*a*) You must have a comfortable position and hold properly so that the rifle does not wobble about and is not disturbed when the trigger is released.

(*b*) You must aim correctly.

(*c*) You must release the trigger in such a way that the aim is not disturbed.

These three points are the three essentials of accurate shooting. Their order of importance is as shown above.

If you cannot hold properly, the other two things correctly done will be of no use to you. Similarly, if you cannot aim correctly good holding and good trigger release will only allow you to hit what you actually aim at. Lastly, if you hold efficiently you will not be able to do much harm to your correct aim by releasing your trigger badly.

We will now take these three essentials in turn, dealing at the moment only with the lying position.

5. Position and Holding. Think of a rifle in a vice. If you take a hearty pull at the trigger with the rifle securely fixed, you will not move the rifle. What you have got to do is to learn to be the vice for your rifle. The best way to do this is to follow these instructions:

(*a*) You must be comfortable. Not all the text-book rules in the world will get you to shoot well if you are uncomfortable.

(*b*) Try and get your comfortable position to copy, as far as possible, that shown in Figures 5 and 6. In Figure 6, A is the left elbow, B the right elbow, and C the spot where the centre of the chest first touches the ground.

The position is based on two triangles, on both of which two of the sides are equal, and the third side as nearly equal as the human body will allow, and as makes no matter. The common practice of trying to put the left elbow underneath the rifle will produce a triangle like that in Figure 7.

This besides being uncomfortable to most people, is mechanically unsound. The whole position is lop-sided. Try pencilling in on a piece of tissue or tracing paper, placed over Figure 6, the altered positions of A, B and C. If A is put underneath the rifle B must come into the left as well, in relation to the rifle; the result is that the whole body is raised and C must go further back towards the waist. See what it looks like when compared with the original triangle suggested.

You will have noticed that the body is at nearly 45° to the line of fire. Try and get your heels flat on the ground and, in effect, almost freeze on to the ground with your knees and elbows. Do not simply lie on the ground as a passenger.

(c) Try and hold the rifle as shown in Figure 8. This is explained below. Starting from the butt end:

    (i) Get the butt firmly bedded either in the shoulder, on the crown of the shoulder or on the top of the forearm, whichever is most comfortable.

    (ii) Press your chin firmly against the butt. This is essential. If, when aiming, you try and keep your head upright, you cannot fail to press hard, and so hold firmly, with your chin. To an on looker your face may look a bit cockeyed and your mouth may even be open, but your chin will be doing its job.

    (iii) Pull the rifle firmly back against the shoulder or arm with your right hand. Don't exaggerate this or your wrist muscles will quiver like an overtaut violin string and your rifle will follow suit. Your right hand should grip the small of the butt so firmly that no extra pressure can be applied. The thumb should be wrapped round the "small" and should not lie on top. The forefinger should be round the trigger and must be free to move independently.

    (iv) The left hand should grasp the rifle as far forward as is comfortable and should hold firmly, but not so firmly as to make the wrist muscles quiver – see (iii) above. A good way of avoiding any tendency to do this is to try to twist the rifle out of the shoulder by a turning pressure with the hand, i.e. push to the right with the ball of the thumb and pull to the left with the forefinger.

    Note. The four single arrows show points of "static" resistance, i.e. the rifle cannot move against the arrow because the bit of the body named prevents it, even though no force is being exerted. The double arrows indicat e pressure which has to be applied.

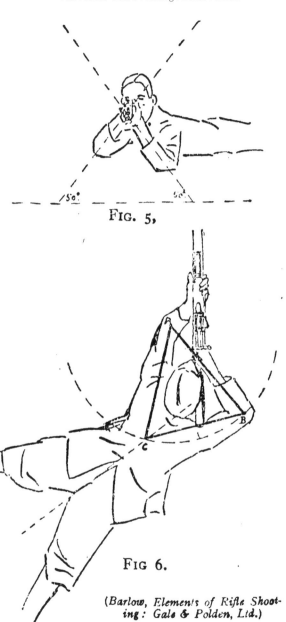

FIG. 5,

FIG 6.

(*Barlow, Elements of Rifle Shooting : Gale & Polden, Ltd.*)

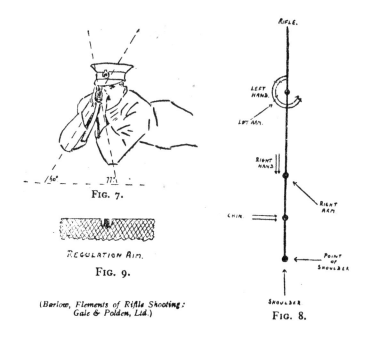

FIG. 7.

REGULATION AIM.

FIG. 9.

(Barlow, Elements of Rifle Shooting:
Gale & Polden, Ltd.)

FIG. 8.

6. Aiming. The term "correct aim" is generally misused and has come to mean what is known as the "regulation aim." In actual fact a "correct aim" is one which you mean to take, each aim being the same as the one before it and the one after it.

Within reason, it doesn't matter what sort of an aim you take provided you always do the same thing and that you know what difference it makes to the sighting of the rifle if you depart from the regulation type.

On the rifles already mentioned, there are two different types of sight, viz:

(*a*) Open.   (*b*) Aperture.

Note. When aiming with either an open or an aperture sight, you will probably find it of assistance to close the disengaged eye (left for a right-handed firer and vice-versa). In actual fact if your aiming eye is the master eye, it won't matter if you leave the other eye open. You will have to close the disengaged eye if you have "neutral vision" (i.e. both eyes equal) or if the eye you aim with is not the master eye. In nine cases out of ten the right eye is the master.

A picture of a regulation aim with an open sight is shown in Figure 9. Instructions are as follows:

(*a*) You must get the foresight in the centre of the U or V of the backsight.

(*b*) Get the tip of the foresight in line with the shoulders of the backsight.

(*c*) Get the tip of the foresight aimed at the point you want to hit.

(*d*) Focus the FORESIGHT.

An aperture sight is easier to aim with than an open sight. The picture that you should see is shown in Figure 10. The rules of aiming with an aperture sight are simply these:

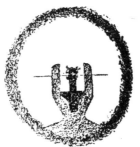

FIG. 10.

(*a*) Look through the aperture and forget about it. The foresight will be centred automatically by the eye. Do not attempt to see the aperture or try to get the foresight in the middle of it. It will get there without your worrying about it if you merely look THROUGH the hole.

(*b*) Focus the FORESIGHT and see this as clearly as your eyesight permits.

(*c*) Put the tip of the foresight on the bottom of the point you want to hit. It doesn't matter if your target is blurred or indistinct. Believe it or not, you will hit it just the same if you hold correctly and merely use a gentle movement of your forefinger alone to release the trigger.

By focusing the foresight rather than the target, any error made in aiming is less severe. For example, if your foresight is blurred and you make a mistake in aiming, that error will be multiplied some hundreds of times on the target, i.e. the number of times that the sight base (distance between foresight and backsight) goes into the range. If on the other hand the foresight is clear and the target blurred the amount of error will only be the amount the aim is wrong on the target. This is relatively small.

Lastly, you must practise to be able to take an accurate aim in the shortest possible time. For deliberate shooting you should never take more than five seconds to get your aim correct. In war, when all targets are of a snapshooting type you must train yourself to do it more quickly still. Try and take a good aim in about two seconds. You can do this by empty rifle practise on the floor of your sitting-room; in other words, drill yourself into it. To get the maximum benefit you must fire as soon as the aim is good. We will therefore pass on to the question of trigger release.

7. Trigger Release. It is hoped that enough has already been said about holding to have impressed on you the absolute necessity for such a tight grip with the right hand that no movement of the trigger finger can cause any further tightening of the hand as you release the trigger. If you have understood this and can do it, trigger release will present no difficulties for you.

All trigger control is dependent on good holding, whether it be trigger pulling or trigger squeezing. The trouble is that most people look at the business the wrong way round and try to make up for bad holding by super "trigger squeezing."

You may have noticed that up to the above paragraph the words "squeezing" or "trigger pressing" have not been mentioned. Many instructors tell people to squeeze a trigger like a sponge. This is absolutely and completely misleading. You cannot squeeze a sponge with one finger only, keeping the remainder of the hand doing nothing. If you squeeze with your whole hand you are bound to move the rifle and that is just what you must avoid doing.

As already stated, the thumb and the remaining three fingers of the right hand should already be gripping the small of the butt so tightly that no further increase of pressure in the form of a squeeze is possible.

Another point is that squeezing takes time and in war you have no time. You must be able to come up, aim and let the shot go in about two seconds. Don't believe the man who says he squeezes in those conditions.

There are two pressures on all the rifles with which you are likely to be armed, i.e. those mentioned at the head of this article. The first pressure must be taken as soon as you bring the rifle into the shoulder. The trigger should be finally released the instant that aim is correct.

Two more small points remain to be mentioned. These are:

(*a*) Use the bony part between the first and second joints to release the trigger. This is the least sensitive part of the finger and if there is a slight drag on the trigger you won't be so likely to notice it. For good, quick, and accurate shooting one doesn't want to feel a drag. Incidentally one gets more leverage by using this part of the finger in preference to the first joint.

(*b*) Gently restrain your breathing at the moment of releasing the trigger. This should become an unconscious action after a time.

8. Rapid Fire. The secret of efficient rapid fire is to have a good bolt manipulation. To a listener the sound of the bolt being opened and closed should come as one sound and not two or four, i.e. "clickety-click" and not "click-clock" nor "cer-lick-cer-lock." The best way to practise this is to lie on your sitting-room floor and drill yourself into reloading smartly with the rifle rested on the ground in front of you. Reload with a flick of the right wrist. Try to break, or flick, the bolt-head off the bolt with a quick flick of the wrist. When you have got the "one sound" movement correctly like this, try reloading with the butt kept in the shoulder. You will find it awkward at first, but drill will soon make it easier. After each reloading motion with the rifle in the shoulder, take the first pressure. In this way you will learn efficient trigger control. As a third stage in learning rapid bolt manipulation, reload and actually go through the action of firing.

Here are some hints to help you:

(*a*) The bolt and bolt-way must be clean and slightly oiled.

(*b*) You must always hold firmly with the left hand while reloading – in the same manner as indicated in 5 (iv) above.

(*c*) You must have a vice-like grip with the right hand and use your chin when firing each shot, in order not to let your trigger finger run away with you in your hurry (i.e. run the whole show).

(*d*) Tilt the rifle slightly to the right when reloading. This will assist rapid bolt action by making the unloading action easier. Similarly bring the rifle back to the upright position as you close the bolt.

(*e*) Keep your head well back from the cocking-piece so that you do not have to move your head unduly when reloading.

(*f*) Always count the number of rounds as you fire and reload when the magazine is empty. Rely on your counting and do not look to see if it's empty!

If you have one, you will find the S.M.L.E. the easiest rifle with which to do rapid fire – it is the best active service rifle in the world. The Springfield you will probably find the next easiest, the other three all being rather more difficult.

9. War shooting in Various Positions. Generally you will find you are either in a trench or in a fold in the ground. You may not be able to get quite the position you would like. You must, however, try and make yourself as comfortable as possible. This can certainly be done when you are in a prepared trench by arranging the sandbag properly.

If you have to fire standing in the open, the following hints may be of use:

(*a*) Push your left arm out absolutely straight and grip the rifle as far forward as possible.

(*b*) Twist the rifle to the right with this hand, pushing over to the right with the thumb and pulling under to the left with the fingers.

(*c*) Twist the small of the butt to the left with the right hand.

(*d*) Start aiming just below the thing you want to hit and let the shot go when the foresight comes up to it. This is another reason why you can't afford to squeeze your trigger. You simply haven't got time.

When shooting kneeling, try and do as much of the above as possible. You won't be able to get the left arm out straight, but get it as far forward as you can.

CHAPTER 6

SMALL ARMS

Shortages and the need to supply the regular army left the Home Guard reliant initially on personal firearms, whether World War I vintage service revolvers, shotguns or hunting rifles. When firearms were initially supplied by the government, they were a mixture of standard Lee-Enfield rifles and some P.14. 303-in. rifles. From mid-1940 these were largely replaced by US manufactured M1917 Enfield rifles. These were supplemented by M1918 Browning Automatic Rifles, World War I issue Lewis Guns and Browning machine guns and from 1941 by Thompson sub-machine guns. It is clear from even this short list that Home Guard volunteers were required to be competent with a number of different firearms. Added to this was the expectation that, in the case of invasion, they would be capable of turning the enemy's weaponry against him. Home Guard training manuals thus often contained detailed specifications on a wide range of Allied and Axis weapons. Those included in this chapter are only a sample of those detailed in the *Small Arms Manual* written by J. A. Barlow and Lt. Col. R. E. W. Johnson of the London Rifle Brigade. This was first published in January 1942 and is again typical of the private publications that supplemented official Ministry material.

Small Arms Manual (1942)

SMALL ARMS

INTRODUCTION

Large numbers of various types and kinds of small-arms weapons are in use in the present war by the Royal Navy, the Army, the Royal Air Force, and the Home Guard. These consist of our own standard and reserve patterns of Rifles, Machine-guns, Light Machine-guns, Machine carbines, and Pistols, together with many different varieties and calibres of similar weapons from the U.S.A.

It may fall to the lot of anyone in any of the services in battle to require to know how to use any particular one of the various weapons with which he may possibly come in contact.

It must be remembered that the man on service may also have the opportunity of employing captured weapons against the enemy. This adds to the extent of the knowledge necessary for the man in the services who desires to make himself an efficient "man-at-arms".

This little book, therefore, has been produced with the intention of summarizing the main items of requisite knowledge about each of the following weapons:

(i) Our own small arm weapons.

(ii) U.S.A. small-arm weapons procured by Great Britain, and

(iii) Similar enemy weapons of which sufficient information is available.

The service man possessing only an elementary knowledge of any particular rifle or light machine-gun should, from the information contained herein, be able to utilize any of the other types in battle.

In addition to the mechanical information given in the body of the book it appears desirable to touch briefly, in this introduction, on the rôles for which the various types of weapons are designed in order to clear away any misconceptions which may arise as to their comparative efficiency. For example, in the case of rifles the extreme range is very much greater than the maximum *accurate* range, whilst with the Medium Machine-Gun the difference between the extreme range and the maximum accurate range is far smaller.

Brief notes on the functions in battle of the weapons are therefore given below.

The Rifle.

This is the personal weapon of the great majority of soldiers. It is often alluded to, and rightly so, as the "soldier's best friend," and if properly cared for and handled is a powerful weapon of offence or defence at all ranges from point blank to at least 600 yards. Between 600 and about 1,000 yards only a skilled marksman can be expected to hit individual men, although in countries where the atmosphere is clear and visibility is exceptionally good hits have been recorded at distances up to one mile.

At ranges up to about 400 yards the trajectory of the bullet is so flat that a man who knows his rifle should have no difficulty in hitting his opponent, using the battle sight (where provided) without having to aim down more than a very few inches at any distance.

The principle of "lengthening the bayonet" by firing from the hip during an assault with the bayonet should not be forgotten, but practice will be necessary to acquire accuracy with this method as there is a very marked tendency to shoot high.

Although the greater number of L.M.G.s now issued have to some extent minimised the necessity for accurate rapid fire, the ability to produce such fire is still a most valuable attribute of the rifle, particularly in the case of the No. 1 (S.M.L.E.) and No. 4 rifles, both of which have the famous Lee bolt action. Soldiers armed with either of these should have no difficulty in attaining, with practice, a speed of anything up to twenty aimed shots in one minute, whilst those armed with the No. 3 (P. 14) or the U.S.A. Model 1917 should be able to reach fifteen rounds a minute.

Ability to fire quickly at a fleeting target (i.e. Snapshooting) should also be encouraged. To be able to bring the rifle into the shoulder and the sights into instant alignment, combined with the ability to get the shot away accurately and at once in any circumstances, will give the soldier a very marked advantage over a less skilled opponent.

The Light Machine-Gun.

This weapon is the main armament of the Infantry section and its fire will normally be controlled by the section commander. Although the man who carries and fires it may have no other arms it cannot be strictly regarded as a "personal" weapon since any man in the section may be called upon to use it at a moment's notice, and since it is not as handy as a rifle, on account of its greater weight, for use at close quarters or on the move.

Its weight, however, coupled with the fact that it is normally supported at the forward end by a bipod (i.e. not solely supported by the firer) make it reasonably accurate at distances greater than could be achieved with the rifle, although it uses the same ammunition. The average man can expect to produce fire effect with the modern L.M.G. at ranges up to 800 or 1,000 yards, depending on visibility, and the expert may be able to deliver the goods at even greater ranges.

With some L.M.G.s it is possible to fire either single shots or bursts; with others bursts only are possible. Bursts should be of about four or five rounds.

If it is possible to fire the weapon from a tripod mounting, accurate fire can be brought to bear on suitable targets such as bridges and defiles at ranges up to 1,500 yards or more. At any range in excess of 600 yards fire will normally be in bursts and not in single shots.

The Medium Machine-Gun.

Since this weapon is normally mounted on a heavy tripod its accuracy can be relied upon at ranges considerably greater than those attained by the L.M.G. or the rifle. In the case of the Vickers gun this increase in accurate range is enhanced by the fact that special (Mark VIII) ammunition is used which makes it possible to employ the gun in a miniature artillery role at ranges up to 4,500 yards.

The medium machine-gun should, therefore, not be wasted on short-range tasks which can be undertaken with L.M.Gs. (or, even by riflemen), but should be used on targets at ranges in excess of 1,000 yards. Fire should be in bursts of not less than 20 rounds, the length of burst increasing with the ranges up to about 30 rounds.

The Machine Carbine.

Next to the rifle as a personal weapon comes the "Tommy gun," and used intelligently it is a very fine weapon for either offence or defence, but it has a grave limitation in the fact that its accuracy deteriorates rapidly at ranges greater than about 100 to 150 yards. This on account of the small charge behind the bullet – with a consequent low muzzle velocity – and the short barrel. The machine carbine is basically a weapon of opportunity and cannot take the place of the L.M.G. or even the rifle except at very short ranges where its handiness and capability of producing a good volume of fire quickly make it eminently suitable for patrols and street fighting.

This weapon must not be regarded as a "bullet-spray"; economy of ammunition must constantly be emphasized. The correct way to use it is to fire the shortest burst which will achieve the desired result, and to strive to make every shot tell.

The Pistol.

Revolvers and Automatic Pistols are essentially personal weapons and their main role should be defence rather than attack, although its value as a weapon of offence in the hands of a determined and experienced man must not be under-rated. Whilst experts can do considerable damage with such weapons at ranges of about 50 yards the average user will not have much success even on a life-size figure target at any range of much more than as many feet. More-over, to achieve anything like accuracy, combined with the speed which will usually be essential, considerable practice will be necessary. This also applies very forcibly to any attempt to shoot from the hip with the pistol, which should be strongly discouraged on the ground that it inevitably results in waste of ammunition, until the firer is reasonably proficient in the more normal position with the arm raised.

SECTION I

RIFLES

Preliminary Note.

Any man in any of the regular services or in the Home Guard will know how to use at least one rifle, i.e. the type with which he or his unit is armed. All rifles are very much alike in essentials, although they all have certain individual peculiarities. Therefore little additional knowledge is required to be able to utilize any other type which may be encountered.

This chapter will therefore merely furnish:

(*a*) Brief particulars of each rifle;

(*b*) Information as to how to remove and replace bolt and magazine;

(*c*) Description of mechanical safety device, if any; and

(*d*) Any special features of the particular rifle under review.

In view of the fact that removal and replacement of the bolt and magazine is really all that anyone need be able to do, no attempt has been made to cover detailed stripping. Such stripping is a matter for the armourer.

1. .303-INCH SHORT MAGAZINE LEE-ENFIELD (S.M.L.E.), Mks. III AND III*.

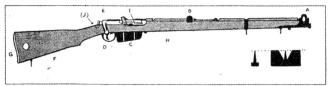

Fig. 1.—The modern Service rifle.

(A) Foresight and lugs; **(B)** Backsight; **(C)** Magazine; **(D)** Trigger-guard and trigger; **(E)** Bolt and breech mechanism; **(H)** Point of balance; **(I)** Cut-out; **(J)** Safety-catch; **(F)** Butt; **(G)** Heel-plate.

(a) Particulars.

Service designation.	Rifle No. 1 Mks. III and III*.
Weight.	8 lbs.10½ ozs.
Weight with bayonet.	9 lbs. 11½ ozs.
Length with normal butt.	3 ft. 8½ ins.
Length with bayonet	5 ft. 1½ ins.
Capacity of magazine.	10 rounds.

Charger or clip loading	Charger (5 rounds).
Type of sights.	Open. U notch and blade.
Range of adjustment.	200 to 2,000 yds.
Cut-off for magazine.	Mk. III – yes. Mk. III* – no.

(b) Removal and replacement of bolt and magazine.

(i) To remove bolt.

Push forward the safety-catch which will be found on the left side at the rear of the action. Raise the bolt-lever by pulling it up to the left, and pull the bolt back as far as it will come. Place your right thumb on the left of the bridge charger guide and hook the forefinger under bolt-head. Levering against the thumb, pull up the bolt-head. This action will release it from the spring retaining-catch. See that the bolt-head is in line with the bolt-way in the rear of the body and withdraw bolt.

*Note. Before attempting to lever up the bolt-head over its retaining catch make sure that the bolt is fully to the rear.

(ii) To replace bolt.

All bolts are numbered to coincide with the number of the rifle to which they belong. Make sure that you are putting back the correct bolt before you start. A wrong bolt, which will most probably fit badly, gives inaccurate shooting.

Reverse the process outlined in (i) above, but before doing so make sure:

(a) That the bolt-head is fully screwed home;

(b) That the cocking-piece is in line with the lug on the underside of the bolt; and

(c) That, before forcing the bolt-head down over the spring retaining-catch, the bolt is pulled back to the fullest extent, i.e. until the bolt-head is touching the resistance shoulder on the top right rear of the body.

(iii) To remove magazine.

Push in, or pull up, the magazine-catch which is just in front of the trigger. Remove the magazine.

(iv) To replace magazine.

Push the magazine into the magazine opening with the narrower end first and pointing forwards. Snap home and test that the magazine-catch is properly engaged by trying to pull the magazine out.

(v) To remove magazine platform and spring for cleaning.

Hold the magazine in your right hand, platform upper-most. Push the rear of the magazine platform down into the magazine casing with the thumb of the left hand, and ease the front of the platform up behind the two lips of the magazine. Withdraw platform and spring.

(vi) To replace magazine platform and spring.

Insert spring in casing. Push down rear of platform and lever under the two rear lips of the magazine. Continue the downward pressure until you can lever the front of the platform under the two front lips. Relax pressure and the platform will rise into place. If it does not do so, give a light push downwards on the front end of the platform. This will rectify the jam which will have been caused by the platform binding against the forward internal ribs of the magazine casing.

(c) Applied and mechanical safety devices.

(i) Applied safety.

Safety-catch on the left rear side of the action. When pushed forward, it is out of action. In this condition the bolt can be operated and the rifle fired. When pulled fully back to the rear, the locking-bolt of the safety-catch protrudes into the short cam slot at the rear of the bolt, thus preventing rotation of the bolt. At the same time the half-moon lug of the safety-catch engages in one of two recesses in the cocking- piece, thus stopping forward or rearward movement of the latter. When in the fired position, the rear recess is engaged; in the cocked position the forward recess is utilised.

(ii) Mechanical safety.

If the bolt is not correctly closed when the trigger is released, one of two things will happen, viz. either:

(*a*) The bolt will be forced into the closed position by the cocking-piece going forwards, or

(*b*) The action will go into *half-cock*.

The half-cock position is brought about as follows: With the bolt so far from being closed that it will not respond as in (a) above, the stud on the cocking-piece jams behind the stud which lies between the long and short cam grooves on the bolt. On releasing the trigger the sear rises, and on pushing down the bolt-lever the cocking-piece is freed from interference with the stud on the bolt, flying forward under the influence of the striker spring until it is again held up, this time by the engagement of its half-bent with the sear.

The half-bent being undercut, the trigger is locked; at the same time the stud on the cocking-piece is now in the long cam groove in the bolt and lying immediately alongside the stud dividing the short and long grooves, and therefore the bolt-lever cannot be rotated and the action opened.

To *remedy* when the bolt goes into *half-cock*, pull back the cocking-piece by hand to full-cock. No other action is possible.

(d) Special features.

The locking-lugs on the Lee-Enfield action are at the rear of the bolt. One lug bears against the resistance shoulder on the right of the body, while the other rides up, and bears against, the rear wall of a cam slot on the left side of the body.

This system of locking has both advantages and disadvantages. From the rough wear and tear service point of view, the former outweigh the latter. The main disadvantage is that super-accuracy is difficult to obtain since the bolt and the major portion of the body is in a state of compression when the shot is fired. Accuracy, however, is sufficiently good from the service point of view, with the sole exception of sniping. This drawback is amply compensated for by the following advantages:

  (i) Simple, sweet, and easy bolt action which is admirable for rapid fire. There is no abrupt turn over of the bolt-lever such as is necessitated by front locking-lugs.

 (ii) Able to function well in adverse conditions of sand, dust, mud, etc.

(iii) Easy to clean, owing to the absence of forward locking recesses in the body.

This action is quite the best in the world for ordinary rough wear and tear of service conditions.

2. .303-INCH PATTERN '14. (P.14.).

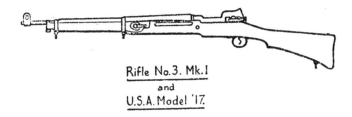

Rifle No.3. Mk.I
and
U.S.A. Model '17.

(a) Particulars.

Service designation.	Rifle No. 3 Mk. I*.
Weight.	9 lbs. 6 ozs.
Weight with bayonet.	10 lbs. 7 ozs.
Length with normal butt.	3 ft. 10½ ins.
Length with bayonet.	5 ft. 3¼ ins.
Capacity of magazine.	5 rounds.
Charger or clip loading	Charger (5 rounds).
Type of sights.	Aperture.
Range of adjustment.	200 to 1,650 yds.
	There is also a battle sight (aperture) sighted for 400 yds.
Cut-off for magazine.	Nil.

(b) Removal and replacement of the bolt and magazine.

(i) To remove the bolt.

Push forward the safety-catch which will be found on the right-hand side at the rear of the body behind the bolt-lever. Raise the bolt-lever upwards to the left and pull the bolt to the rear. With the left thumb push out the bolt retaining catch on the left of the body to the left and withdraw the bolt.

(ii) To replace bolt.

Before attempting to replace the bolt ensure

(*a*) That the tooth on the front end of the cocking-piece is engaged in the short groove on the end of the bolt, and

(*b*) That the extractor is in direct line with the solid lug on the right of the bolt.

3. .303-INCH RIFLE No. 4.

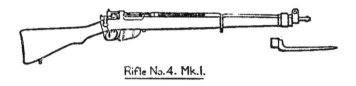

Rifle No.4. Mk.1.

(a) Particulars.

Service designation.	Rifle No. 4 Mk. 1.
Weight.	9 lbs. 3 ozs.
Weight with bayonet.	9 lbs. 10 ozs.
Length with normal butt.	3 ft. 8¾ ins.
Length with bayonet.	4 ft. 5 ins. (approx.).
Capacity of magazine.	10 rounds.
Charger or clip loading.	Charger (5 rounds).
Type of sights.	Aperture and blade.
Range of adjustment.	Early models, 200-1,300 yds.
	Production models, 100-600 yds.
Cut-off.	Early models – Yes.
	Production models – No.

N.B. The bayonet is of a new pattern, or rather a resuscitation of an old type. It is a spike bayonet of comparatively short length, about 8 ins. long. This makes for lightness and handiness which more than make up for what is lost in length of reach.

General description.

This rifle differs very little from the S.M.L.E., of which it is a modern copy. In fact when it was first produced it was known as the S.M.L.E. Mk. VI.

The S.M.L.E., as it is generally known, is not designed in any way for modern mass production, having been born many years before such things were thought of. The Rifle No. 4 was designed purely from the point of view of mass production. The number of different types of steel and of difficult machining operations has been reduced to a minimum. At the same time certain improvements have been incorporated. These are:

 (i) The lighter and shorter and more easily manufactured bayonet.

 (ii) Slightly heavier and sturdier barrel, which makes for greater accuracy.

 (iii) Improved stocking up arrangements, including a better form of nose cap, which also helps to give greater accuracy.

(iv) A machined surface for the bolt-head to ride upon inside the body.

 (v) A smaller and more compact bolt-head (permitted by (iv) above).

(vi) A new type of bolt retaining arrangement.

(vii) An aperture instead of an open sight. This again improves accuracy.

(viii) The bayonet is fitted by means of a turning lock. This also is a reversion to a design of a century or more ago.

A few thousand rifles were made up for troop trials round about 1930-31. These proving satisfactory, the design was approved and laid aside for use in emergency, since financial stringency prevented any more positive action being taken at that time. Since the outbreak of the present war a few further modifications to the design have taken place in order to assist manufacture. It is probable that substantial numbers of the later design will be manufactured in the near future. There will thus be two models in existence

(b) Removal and replacement of bolt and magazine.

(i) To remove bolt.

(*a*) Early Models. Open the bolt as for the S.M.L.E., but do not draw it right back. Depress the catch in front of the resistance shoulder and, while keeping it depressed, draw back the bolt to the fullest extent. Leave go of the catch, push up the bolt-head, and withdraw the bolt.

(*b*) Production Models. Raise the bolt-lever as for the S.M.L.E., but only draw back the bolt about half an inch until the gap in the bolt-head runner on the body coincides with the bolt-head itself. In this position lift up the bolt- head into the vertical position and withdraw the bolt.

(ii) To replace bolt.

(*a*) Early Models. See that the bolt-head is screwed home. Place the bolt in the bolt-way and push forward. Turn the bold-head down, pressing it against the spring retaining-catch; at the same time push the bolt forward and home. The retaining-catch will rise behind the bolt-head as soon as the latter is clear.

(*b*) Production Models. See that the bolt-head is screwed home. Place the bolt in the bolt-way and push forward. When the bolt-head is past the bridge charger guide, turn it over to the right until it rests on the runner on the body. Position the bolt-head over the cut-away portion of the runner and push down and forwards.

(iii) Removal and replacement of the magazine and magazine platform.

Identical with the S.M.L.E.

(c) Applied and mechanical safety devices.

Both the applied and mechanical safety are exactly the same as in the S.M.L.E.

(d) Special features and general information of interest.

These are tabulated, in this instance, in the general description under (*a*) above.

Advantage has been taken of the opportunity afforded by war production, in which time is a vital factor, to dispense with a certain number of peace-time frills. These are the modifications referred to in the general description under (a). The main modifications are:

(i) Omission of $\left\{\begin{array}{l}\text{cut-off.} \\ \text{piling swivel.} \\ \text{butt disc.}\end{array}\right.$

(ii) Simplified design of foresight protector.

(iii) Radically simplified backsight.

(iv) Circular spike bayonet vice cruciform.

(v) Further simplified bolt retaining arrangements.

A brief description of items (iii) and (v) above are as follows:

SIMPLIFIED BACKSIGHT

This sight consists simply of two aperture battle sights set at right angles to one another. The shorter range one is calibrated for 300 yards when the bayonet is fixed and is correct for 400 yards when the bayonet is not fixed. The longer range one is correct for 600 yards – of course without the bayonet.

Presupposing that the normal practice of fixing bayonets when within 300 yards of the enemy is adhered to, the method of use is as follows:

(i) At 300 yards use the 300 aperture with the bayonet fixed and take a normal aim.

(ii) At 400 yards use the 300 aperture without the bayonet fixed and take a normal aim.

(iii) At 600 yards use the 600 aperture (obviously without the bayonet fixed) and take a normal aim.

(iv) Up to 300 yards aim down a little, using the 300 aperture. The maximum amount of "aim down" at any intermediate range does not exceed 8 inches.

(v) At 500 yards or thereabouts use the 600 aperture and aim down. The amount of "aim down" at 500 yards is at the most 2½ feet.

The above rules are very simple, and ensure that the man always keeps his target in view. They also obviate any possibility that a man will forget to alter his sights as the range alters. He has to use his head a little but all that he has to do, somewhere between 400 and 500 yards is to flip one sight down and the other comes up automatically.

SIMPLIFIED BOLT RETAINING ARRANGEMENTS

These consist simply of the abolition of the bolt-head catch and the substitution for it of a small cut-away in the bolt-head runner in the body. The bolt-head will only come out of the body when it strictly coincides with this "cut-away."

4. .303-INCH CANADIAN ROSS RIFLE.

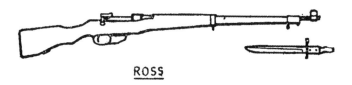

ROSS

(a) Particulars.

Service designation	Ross rifle .303-in. Mk. III B.
Weight	9 lbs. 14 ozs.
Weight with bayonet.	11 lbs
Length.	4 ft. 2½ ins.
Length with bayonet.	5 ft. 0½ ins.
Capacity of magazine.	5 rounds.
Charger or clip loading	Charger
Type of sights.	Aperture and semi-open.
Range of adjustment	Aperture 200 to 1,200 yds. Battle sight (semi-open) 400 yds. Long-range sight (semi-open), 1,000 to 1,600 yds.
Cut-off for magazine.	Yes.

(b) Removal and replacement of bolt.

(i) To remove the bolt.

The safety-catch on this rifle is on the right side on the bolt-lever. It is a catch of the swing over type, on which is stamped on either side the words "READY" and "SAFE." Put the catch to the "READY" position.

On the left side of the body you will find a thumb-piece which can be turned, in the vertical plane, to three positions, i.e. "up", "centre", or "down". Place this thumb-piece in the centre position. This will permit the bolt to be withdrawn.

To withdraw the bolt, pull it straight to the rear by means of the bolt-lever. The bolt action is of the straight pull type and does not belong to the usual class of rotating bolt actions.

(ii) To replace the bolt.

See that the bolt-head lugs are in the same horizontal plane as the bolt-lever. In this position the main spring is compressed and the bolt-head proud of the sleeve by about an inch. It is possible for the bolt-head to spring back against the sleeve under the influence of the main spring. Hence the warning to see that the lugs are in the same horizontal plane as the bolt-lever, i.e. bolt extended and main spring compressed.

With the bolt in this condition insert into the rifle, seeing that the grooves on the bolt and the runners on the body coincide, and push home.

Thereafter put the thumb-piece on the left side to the top position.

Note. The magazine is not made for ready removal from the rifle. There fore no mention will be made here of how to remove or strip. With practice it can be cleaned quite well when in the rifle.

5. U.S.A. MODEL '17. .300-INCH.

(a) Particulars.

Service designation	U.S. Model '17.
Weight.	Approximately the same as
Weight with bayonet.	for the British .303-inch P. '14.
Length.	
Length with bayonet.	
Capacity of magazine.	5 rounds.
Charger of clip loading.	Charger (small brass type).
Type of sights.	
Range of adjustment.	As for British P. '14.
Cut off for magazine.	Nil

(See illustration for .303-inch Pattern '14. (P.14.).)

(b) Removal and replacement of bolt and magazine, etc.

Exactly the same as for the British P. '14.

6. U.S.A. SPRINGFIELD. .300-INCH.

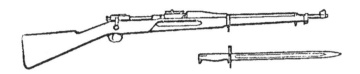

U.S.A. Springfield Model '03.

(a) Particulars.

Service designation.	U.S. .300-inch Springfield. Model 1903.
Weight.	9 lbs. 11 ozs.
Weight with bayonet.	10 lbs. 11 ozs.
Length	3 ft. 7¼ ins.
Length with bayonet.	4 ft. 11 ins. (approx.).
Charger or clip loading.	Charger (small brass type).
Type of sights.	Aperture and open. (See below under (d).
Range of adjustment	100 to 2,850 yds.
Cut-off for magazine.	Yes. Same type as the Ross.

(b) Removal and replacement of bolt and magazine

(i) To remove bolt.

Place cut-off in centre position as for the Ross. Raise the bolt-lever and withdraw the bolt.

(ii) To replace bolt.

With the cut-off in the centre position, hold the rifle in the fingers of the left hand with the thumb extending over the left side of the body. Then, while pressing down the magazine platform with the thumb of the left hand, slide the bolt into the bolt-way in the body. Lower the bolt-lever, turn the safety-catch and cut-off down to the left, and pull the trigger to release the springs.

(iii) To remove the magazine platform, spring, and bottom plate.

Proceed as for the P. '14.

(iv) To assemble magazine platform, spring, and bottom plate.

As for the P. '14.

(c) Applied and mechanical safety devices.

(i) Applied safety.

Safety-catch on the rear of the bolt, working laterally. It operates in three positions as follows:

1. When turned to the *right* (which can only be done when the rifle is cocked) the catch is in action and the rifle is at "*safe*".
2. When turned into the vertical position, the bolt may be stripped by unscrewing the cocking-piece and assembly from the body of the bolt.
3. When turned to the *left*, the catch is inoperative, the bolt may be manipulated, and the rifle fired.

(ii) Mechanical safety.

If the bolt is not properly closed, the cam on the cocking-piece will strike the cocking-cam on the bolt, and the energy of the main spring will be expended in closing the bolt, instead of in striking the cap of the cartridge. This prevents the possibility of the cartridge being fired until the bolt is fully closed. Obviously a miss-fire may result.

(d) Special features and general information.

This rifle is the only service rifle which attempts to correct for drift, i.e. the lateral movement of the bullet set up by the twist of the rifling. Drift for service purposes is an un-important item since the amount is negligible when compared with the wind and other factors. A description of the back sight is as follows:

The leaf is graduated from 100 to 2,850 yards. The lines extending across one or both side of the leaf are 100-yard divisions, while the longer of the short lines are 50-yard, and the shorter lines 25-yard divisions.

The drift slide is attached to the slide proper. The latter has a small aperture near the base, a triangular opening with an open sighting notch, and another open sighting notch in its upper edge. As the slide is moved up the scale, so it is moved over to the left by the drift slide, thus automatically compensating for drift.

With leaf up, ranges from 100 to 2,350 yards can be obtained through the aperture; from 100 to 2,450 through the open notch at the bottom of the triangular opening; and from 1,400 top 2.750 yards through the open sighting notch in the upper edge. The 2,850-yard range is obtained through the open notch in the upper end of the leaf itself.

With leaf down there is a battle sight which is calibrated for 530 yards.

7. 300-INCH BROWNING AUTO RIFLE.

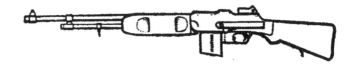

BROWNING LIGHT AUTO RIFLE

(a) Particulars.

Service designation.	.300-inch Browning Auto Rifle.
Weight.	15 lbs. 12 ozs.
Length.	3 ft. 7 ins. approx, (without flash reducer).
Locked or unlocked.	Locked. Rear end of breechblock rises.
Capacity of magazine.	20 rounds.
Charger or clip loading.	Spare magazines are used for replenishment of the rifle, but there is a separate "charger guide" (sometimes called a "magazine filler") by means of which spare magazines can be refilled by utilising the normal brass type of U.S.A. charger holding 5 rounds.
Type of sights.	Aperture.
Range of adjustment.	200-1,600 yards. Battle sight
Cut-off for magazine.	Nil 400 yards.

GENERAL DESCRIPTION

This is a heavy type of automatic rifle, or, if you prefer to call it so, a light type of light machine-gun.

It can fire either single shots or fully automatic bursts. There is a change lever on the left-hand side of the weapon just beside the back of the trigger guard. There are three letters to indicate what happens when the change lever is in each of the three positions:

F. Forward position = Single shots.
A. Centre position = Fully automatic.
S. Rear position = Safe.

There is a small safety stud operated by a spring in between A and S to ensure that the change lever does not slip to "Safe" during firing automatic. This also helps to keep the change lever at "Safe" when it is to the rear.

These weapons take .300-inch ammunition and, like the U.S.A. rifles and Lewis guns, have a red band painted on the body.

The weapon should be rested on cover if possible or else fired in the open like a rifle. *Normally, the weapon should be used for firing single shots, the fully automatic capacity only being employed in an emergency.* Besides avoiding waste of ammunition, this disguises the fact that an automatic weapon is present, until the enemy is too close to do anything about it.

(b) Stripping and Assembly.

(i) To strip.

1. Remove magazine by pressing in catch inside front of trigger guard.
2. Ensure that the rifle is unloaded by pulling back the cocking-handle.
3. Leaving the rifle cocked, rotate retaining pin at left front of body, half turn clockwise and remove.
4. Pull forward handguard complete with gas cylinder and remove.
5. Press the trigger, and control forward movement of action.
6. Turn rifle upside down.
7. Rotate retaining pin on left of trigger guard quarter turn clockwise and remove.

8. 7.92 mm. GERMAN MAUSER.

MAUSER

(a) Particulars.

Weight.	} Less bayonet	{ 9 lbs. 12 ozs.
Length.		4 ft. 4¾ ins.
Capacity of magazine.		5 rounds.
Charger or clip loading.		Charger (small brass type).
Type of sights.		Open V notch and barleycorn.
Range of adjustment.		Graduated 400-2,000 metres
Cut-off for magazine		Nil.

9. .55-INCH BOYS' ANTI-TANK RIFLE.

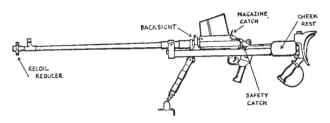

(a) Particulars.

Service designation.	Rifle Boys', Mark I.
Weight.	35½ lbs.
Length.	5 ft. 4 ins.
Feed.	Overhead box magazine.
Magazine capacity.	5 rounds.
Ejection.	Underneath.
Sights.	Aperture.
Range of adjustment.	2 fixed settings – 300 and 500 yds.

(b) Removal and replacement of bolt.

(i) To remove bolt.

Open bolt and depress small catch just beneath the magazine catch. Withdraw the bolt.

(ii) To replace bolt.

Reverse the above.

(c) Loading and unloading.

(i) To fill magazine.

You must be careful to push the base of the round back from in front of the two lips of the magazine. Do not attempt to force the round downwards between the lips.

(ii) To load.

As for Bren.

(iii) To unload.

As for Bren. The magazine catches are of the same type.

(d) Special features of information and interest.

1. The monopod support folds forwards. It is held fast in either the firing or folded position by a strong spring-controlled stud on the right-hand side at the pivot-axis of the monopod. To change from one position to another press in the stud, and place the monopod in the desired position.

2. Safety-catch on left side. "Fire" is forward. "Safe" is with catch turned to rear.

3. In order to speed up production the monopod, which requires considerable machining, has now been superseded by a bipod which, by an ingenious quick-release, can easily be detached from the rifle. This is a great advantage when the weapon is mounted in an A.F.V

SECTION II

LIGHT MACHINE-GUNS

Preliminary.

A light machine-gun is an automatic weapon of rifle calibre which, in its primary rôle, does not require any form of mounting other than a bipod or similar support which is normally attached to it in all circumstances. It is capable of a reasonable amount of sustained fire, though, being air-cooled, its limit of endurance is not so great as that of water-cooled weapons. This, however, is sometimes offset by the possibility of changing the barrel in a matter of a few seconds

Most light machine-guns are magazine-fed, as opposed to being belt-fed the capacity of the magazine varying with the type of weapon and with the task to be undertaken (e.g. magazines larger than normal are used on some weapons for A.A. fire).

Generally speaking a light machine-gun should possess the following virtues:

   (i) Lightness, combined with strength.

 (ii) Simplicity, and ease of stripping in the field.

(iii) Ability to fire either in bursts or in a succession of single shots.

1. .303-INCH BREN L.M.G.

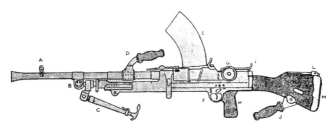

Fig. 6.—The Bren-gun.

(A) Foresight; (B) Gas regulator; (C) Bipod; (D) Carrying handle; (E) Magazine; (F) Trigger and trigger guard; (G) Backsight drum; (H) Pistol grip; (I) Backsight; (J) Butt handle; (K) Butt; (L) Butt strap; (M) Butt plate.

Illustration of the Bren Gun taken from *Home Guard Officers & Section Leaders Handbook* by Alfred Kerr (Hazell, Watson & Viney Ltd., September 1941)

(a) Particulars.

Service designation.	.303-in. Bren, Mk. I and II.
Weight.	23 lbs.
Length.	45½ ins.
System of operation.	Gas-operated.
Locked or unlocked.	Locked by rising rear end of breech-block.
Method of feed.	Box or drum (A.A.) magazine, from above.
Magazine capacity.	Box, 30 rounds; drum (A A.), 100 rounds.
Weight of magazines	
Box: Full	2¾ lbs.
Empty	17 ozs.
Drum: Full	12 lbs. 2 ozs.
Empty	6 lbs. 10 ozs.
Ejection.	Underneath.
Cocking-handle.	Right-hand side.
Condition of breach on:	
(a) Cease fire.	Open.
(b) Empty magazine:	
(i) Box.	Open. Moving parts held back by. projections on rear of magazine platform
(ii) Drum.	Closed.
Types of fire.	Automatic or single shot.
Speed of gun (cyclic rate).	450-550 rounds per minute.
Sights. Type.	Aperture.
Range of adjustment.	{ Mk. I, 200–2,000 (50 yds. clicks). Mk. II, 200–1800.
Ammunition.	Any .303 British Service.
Tripod (for use in rôle of Medium M.G.)	{ Weight, 30 lbs. Traverse limit, 42 degrees. Elevation limit, 19 degrees.

(b) Loading and unloading.

(i) To fill the magazine (box type).

If you have a filler; clip the magazine into the mouth of the filler. Then see that the filling-lever is as far over to the left as it will go. Fill the hopper with about forty rounds. Thereafter push the filling-lever over to its right limit and back to its left limit six times. This will put thirty rounds into the magazine.

Do not hurry or jerk the filling movements. Six steady pushes and pulls are what is required.

If you have to fill by hand, proceed as follows:

(1) Holding the magazine in one hand, opening upwards and horizontal, front end towards you, place a cartridge on the magazine platform so that the cartridge is slightly in front of its final position in the magazine. Press the cartridge down with the thumb of the hand holding the magazine and push it backwards as far as possible with the other hand. Repeat with each round until the magazine is full.

Note. Normally, although the magazine will hold 30 rounds, only 28 will be inserted in order not to overstrain the magazine spring.

(2) Care must be taken in loading to avoid getting the rim of any cartridge behind that of the cartridge next above it (i.e. inserted immediately before it) since this will cause a "rim over rim" stoppage.

Note. The easiest way of sorting out carton-packed ammunition which is packed head to tail is to grab as many rounds as you can in one hand, and then catch hold of as many bases as you are able with the other. You will find that all but one or two are sorted out.

(ii) To fill the magazine (drum type).

Full instructions on the use and handling of the drum type (100-round) magazine will be found on the inside of the lid of the box containing the magazine equipment.

(iii) To load.

1. If shut, push open the magazine opening cover.

2. Take the magazine in the right hand, mouth of the magazine downwards, insert the lip at the front end of the mouth into the magazine opening, hooking it under the front end of the opening; lower the rear of the magazine until the magazine-catch engages on the rib on the magazine.

3. If forward, pull back the cocking-handle as far as possible and push forward again, folding it forward against the body.

(N.B. In Mark II guns the C-H does not fold).

4. Place the change lever (on the left of the body, just above the trigger) at SAFE – i.e. in a vertical position.

(iv) To unload.

1. Press the magazine-catch forward with the base of the palm of the hand, at the same time grasping the magazine and tilting it forward until clear of the magazine-catch. Lift off and place on ground or in pouch or box.

2. If at SAFE, move change lever to A (automatic).

3. Press trigger, cock gun, press trigger again.

4. Close magazine and ejection opening covers.

5. If on the range or undergoing elementary training, stand up and report "gun clear."

(c) Preparation for firing.

1. Dry completely the barrel, the face of the breech-block and the gas-affected parts (i.e. gas cylinder, gas regulator, piston and bipod sleeve).

2. See that the gas regulator is set correctly – the normal setting is the No. 2 hole (i.e. next to smallest).

3. Check assembly by working the moving parts.

4. See that the foresight is tight in its block.

5. Check magazine both before and after loading; before to see that the platform does not stick and that the spring is not damaged, after to ensure that it is correctly loaded.

(d) During firing.

1. Above the change lever (on the left of the gun just above the trigger) will be found the letters A.S.R. on the body. These letters correspond to the three possible positions of the lever and indicate that the mechanism is set for automatic fire, safety or single rounds respectively. This lever may be altered from any position to any other whether the moving parts are forward or back but must not be moved from Safe to Automatic whilst the trigger is pressed, or the gun will not fire.

2. If the gun becomes sluggish during firing it is an indication that more gas is probably needed. This is rectified by altering the gas regulator to the next largest hole.

(e) Points to note after firing.

1. Strip the gun and clean the barrel by first pouring water through it. Boiling water is best, but hot water will do, and even cold water is better than no water at all. Dry and oil up.

2. Clean gas-affected parts by the application of plenty of oil to loosen the fouling. Give the oil a short time to soak in and then wipe clean and dry, finally oiling up. Never scrape fouling off if it can be removed by another method.

3. Be sure not to leave the gun cocked when putting it away – always press the trigger, and ease the working part forward by hand to avoid unnecessary strain.

(f) Stoppages and immediate action.

1. A well cared for gun, with the gas regulator set at the correct hole (normally No. 2) will rarely stop except on account of an empty or a badly filled magazine.

2. In all cases of a stoppage the Immediate Action is:

    (i) pull back cocking-handle.

    (ii) Remove the magazine.

    (iii) Press the trigger.

    (iv) Examine magazine; if empty or badly filled change it.

    (v) Put magazine on and cock gun.

    (vi) Continue firing.

Note. Possible causes: empty magazine, badly filled magazine, missfire, bad ejection, hard extraction.

3. If, after the above sequence, the gun fires a round or two and again stops it is a sign that more gas is wanted and the Immediate Action is:

    (i) Carry out (i), (ii), (iii) and (iv) of paragraph 2.

    (ii) Cock gun (without magazine on).

    (iii) Release barrel, slide forward and change gas regulator to next largest hole.

    (iv) Replace barrel.

    (v) Put magazine on.

    (vi) Continue firing.

Note. Possible causes: insufficient gas, binding of moving parts due to heat or dirt.

(4) If, after the sequence in paragraph 2, the gun will not fire it shows that some mechanical breakdown, either of the gun or the ammunition, has occurred and the Immediate Action is

    (i) Carry out (i) and (ii) of paragraph 2.

    (ii) Examine gun for obstruction and if any is found remove it, replace any broken or damaged parts, and carry on as in (v) and (vi) of paragraph 2.

    (iii) If no obstruction is visible insert clearing plug in breech, press trigger, re-cock gun, thus removing the clearing plug and carry on as in (v) and (vi) of paragraph 2.

Note. Possible causes: broken part, damage to magazine lips, separated case.

(g) Points of interest.

(i) The tripod.

Originally each gun had its own tripod on which it could be used against either ground targets or aircraft. Recently, however, it has been decided that one tripod for every three guns is all that is necessary since the occasions on which it is desirable to use the gun as though it were a medium M.G. are considered to be becoming rarer and rarer.

As an A.A. mounting the tripod leaves a good deal to be desired, and there is now a tendency to abandon it as such and to fire at aircraft from the hip or from a recumbent position. This is quite feasible if tracer ammunition is available, but without such ammunition the problem of hitting a fast-moving aircraft without any means of aiming makes this practice of extremely doubtful value, and the cause of a great and inevitable waste of ammunition.

(ii) The spare barrel.

Each gun has a spare barrel which is carried in the spare parts holdall. After the gun has fired ten magazines at the rapid rate (about three magazines per minute) the barrels should be changed and every effort made to cool the hot one. If possible put the hot barrel in water but at the same time take care to avoid steam blast from the end of the barrel not immersed.

2. LEWIS LIGHT MACHINE-GUN .303-inch British (ground pattern).

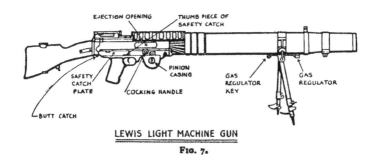

LEWIS LIGHT MACHINE GUN

FIG. 7.

(a) Particulars.

Weight	28 ½ lbs
Length	50 ins
Feed.	Drum magazine actuated by the gun mechanism
Capacity of magazine	47 round
Weight of magazine:	
Empty	1 lb. 12 ozs
Full	4 lbs. 2 ozs
System of operation.	Gas operated
Locked or unlocked.	Locked by rotating bolt
Ejection	Right side
Cocking-handle.	Right-hand side normally
Condition of breech on:	
(a) Cease fire	Open
(b) End of magazine.	Closed
Types of fire	Auto only. No single shot mechanism
Rate of fire (speed of gun)	500–600 rounds per minute

(b) General description.

The gun is the same as was used in the last war and is probably well known to many of you. It has telescopic bipod legs, an aluminium radiator and a casing to assist in keeping the gun cool, normal type of butt and a graduated aperture backsight with range scale up to 2,000 yards. The cocking-handle can be situated either on the right or left-hand side according to the will of the firer. Magazines contain forty-seven rounds.

SIGHTS

Since with this sight, using a correct aim, you will hit what you aim at at 400 yards, you must aim down a little at the shorter ranges because the sight is a fixed one. Suggested simple aims are as follows:

(i) At 400 yards aim at the centre of a man walking or at 6 o'clock at a man lying down.

(ii) At 300 yards and shorter ranges aim at a man's knees. This is about eighteen inches low from the centre of the target. If he is lying down aim about one and a half feet into the ground beneath him.

(c) Loading and Unloading.

(i) To fill magazine.

Put the loading handle in the socket. This releases the magazine catch and allows the centre block to rotate. Put the rounds in one at a time and turn the centre block as you go. Make sure that the groove in the base of the cartridge is engaged in the retaining plates in the magazine. If you have no loading handle press back the magazine catch by hand.

(ii) To load.

1. See that the cocking-handle is forward.

2. Place the magazine on the magazine post.

3. Press the magazine down on to the post until you hear or feel the catch engage.

4. Rotate the magazine clockwise with a pull slap of the palm of the right hand. The reason is that you want to use the same hand both to rotate the magazine and operate the cocking-handle.

5. Pull back the cocking-handle. The gun is now loaded, with a round in the feed way, and bolt to the rear, ready to feed it into the chamber and fire it when the trigger is released.

(iii) To unload.

(a) UNLOADING BY FIRING. Remove the magazine by pressing in the magazine-catch to the right. Raise the butt into the shoulder, release the trigger, cock the gun and again press the trigger.

(b) UNLOADING WITHOUT FIRING. (This will often be necessary when firing on the range.)

Remove the magazine. Press with any suitable object on the base of the round engaged by the feed arm, causing its nose to rise. Pull the round forward as far as possible. Then with one hand controlling the cocking-handle press the trigger and work the cocking-handle forwards and back once or twice until the round falls clear or can be removed by hand. Then carry on as in (*a*) above.

Note, If you have a No. 2, i.e. an assistant for service of the gun, unloading should be done with the butt kept in the shoulder. The No. 1 (firer) presses in the magazine catch, No. 2 pushes up against the centre block of the magazine with his left hand, thus removing it from the post. No. 1 takes the magazine off with his right hand, still holding the butt in the shoulder with the left. The magazine is then passed under the gun to No. 2.

3. 7.92 mm. GERMAN L.M.G. 34.

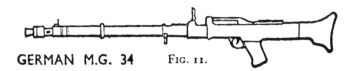

GERMAN M.G. 34   FIG. 11.

(a) Particulars.

Weight.	26 lbs. 2 ozs.
Length.	48 ins.
System of operation	Recoil operated.
Locked or unlocked.	Breech bolt locked to barrel by interrupted threads on bolt head.
Method of feed.	Metal belt (for details see below), fed from left-hand side.
Belts.	Capacity 50 rounds. Metal links joined by coiled wire. The first link in each belt has an opening into which fits a small tag on the end of each belt so that belts of any multiple of 50 rounds may be made up
Ejection.	Underneath.
Cocking-handle.	Right-hand side.
Condition of breech on:	
(*a*) Cease fire.	Open.
(*b*) End of belt.	Closed.
Sights.	Open. A form of optical sight is also carried for use with the tripod.
Range of adjustment.	Open sights, 200–2,000 metres Optical sight, 0–3,000 metres.
Types of fire.	Automatic or single shot.
Speed of gun.	800–900 rounds per minute.

Note. Two variations of the M.G. 34 have recently come to notice.

(*a*) M.G. 34.S. Externally this is very similar to the M.G. 34, but a certain amount of simplification of the working parts has been carried out, probably with a view to assisting production. Rate of fire is the same as for the M.G. 34.

(*b*) M.G. 34/41. This gun is shorter than the M.G. 34, has a heavier barrel and a higher rate of fire which is in the neighbourhood of 1,000 rounds per minute. The working parts are almost identical with those of the M.G. 34.S.

(b) Loading and unloading.

(i) Belt filling.

This is simply a matter of pushing cartridges into the clips until the nib at the end of each clip engages in the groove round the base of the cartridge.

(ii) To load.

The belt is fed into the gun from the left and so that the belt is on top of the cartridges. To load slide forward the cover catch (just in front of the gun butt) and lift the cover. Place the belt in the belt guide so that the right hand cartridge is against the stop on the right side of the guide. Close the cover and pull back the cocking-handle. The gun is now ready to fire.

Note. When closing the cover always ensure that the rib on the feed-actuating-arm is engaged with the slotted stud at the rear of the breech-bolt carrier.

(iii) To unload.

Push forward the cover catch, open the cover and remove the belt. Press the trigger. Close the ejection opening cover.

Note. The ejection opening cover is hinged on the left side of the ejection opening and springs open as soon as the trigger is pressed.

4. 7.92 mm. GERMAN M.G.42.

(a) Particulars.

Weight.	23¾ lbs.
Length.	48 ins.
System of operation.	Recoil operated.
Locked or unlocked.	Breech bolt locked to barrel by roller wedges.

Method of feed.	
Belts.	
Ejection.	
Cocking-handle.	As for M.G.34.
Condition of breech on:	
(*a*) "Cease fire."	
(*b*) End of belt.	

Sights: Types.	As for M.G. 34.
Range of adjustment.	Open sights, 200–2,000 metres
	Optical sight. As for M.G.34.
Type of fire.	Automatic only.
Speed of gun.	About 1,150–1,200 rounds per minute.

(b) Loading and Unloading.

(i) Belt filling.

The belt used is the same as that used with the M.G.34. Each round must be pushed into the belt until the nib at the rear of each clip engages with the extractor groove at the base of the cartridge. Belts of 50 rounds may be joined together by interlocking first and last links and inserting a cartridge.

(ii) To load.

Pull back cocking-handle, push forward breech-cover catch, lift cover and insert belt from left side with belt on top of cartridges so that the first cartridge is against the stop on the right of the feedway, close cover. The gun is now ready to fire.

Note. On closing the cover see that the lug on the top of the breech-block engages in the groove of the feed-actuating-arm.

(iii) To unload.

Push forward the cover-catch, raise the cover and remove the belt. Close the cover, press the trigger and close the ejection-opening cover.

Note. The ejection-opening cover is hinged on the right side of the ejection opening and flies open on the first movement of the breech-block in either direction.

SECTION III

MEDIUM MACHINE-GUNS

1. .303-INCH VICKERS M.G.

(a) Particulars.

Service designation of:

Gun.	.303-inch Vickers M.G. Mk. 1.
Tripod	Mounting tripod. Mk. IV.B.
Weight of gun:	
Without water.	30 lbs. (approx.).
With water.	40 lbs. (approx.).
Length of gun	3 ft. 7½ ins.
System of operation.	Recoil.
Locked or unlocked.	Locked.
Method of locking.	Toggle joint.
Method of feed.	Fabric belt of 250 rounds.
Feed opening.	Right side of feed block and gun.
Ejection.	Underneath.
Speed of gun.	500 rounds per minute.
Service rates of fire.	Rapid – 1 belt per minute Medium – ½ belt per minute Slow – ¼ belt per minute.
Ammunition.	.303-inch Mk. VIII. Z.
Sights.	0 to 4,000 yards.
Type of sight.	Aperture.
Battle sight.	Yes. 400 yards.
Weight of tripod.	50 lbs.

(b) Loading, Firing and Unloading.

(i) To load.

1. Pass tag end of belt through feed block from right and hold this on the other side with left hand.

2. Pull crank handle up and back on to roller.

3. While holding crank handle back, pull belt through feed block to the left as far as it will go.

4. Release crank handle, which will fly forward again under the influence of the fusee spring.

Note 1. The above motions enable the base of the first cartridge in the belt to be gripped by the top of the extractor, preparatory to its being withdrawn from the belt on the next backward movement of the extractor.

5. Repeat motions 2, 3, and 4.

Note 2. The repetition of the initial loading motions performs the following operations:

(i) The extractor withdraws the first round from the belt as the lock comes to the rear.

(ii) The extractor drops when it gets to the end of the cams in the body (if it does not drop, it is forced down by the ramps on the underside of the rear cover).

(iii) The first round is thus presented to the barrel on its correct level and the forward movement of the lock thrusts it into the chamber.

(iv) Just before the lock gets home the side levers, acting on the extractor levers, raise the extractor once more. Since the first round is almost home in the chamber and cannot rise with it, the base of this cartridge rides down the gib on the face of the extractor.

(v) When the extractor has risen to its fullest extent, the firing-pin hole in the bottom of the extractor is opposite the cap of the round in the chamber and the top of the extractor grips the next round in the belt. There are then two live rounds on the face of the extractor, one in the chamber and one in the feed block.

The gun is now fully loaded.

(ii) To fire.

1. Place both hands on the grips with the forefingers on top of the top grip supports, the second fingers on the far side of the safety-catch, and the thumbs on the firing-lever thumb-piece. Do not grasp the grips as if your life depended on it. The gun does not require holding to ensure accuracy – the tripod does the job for you. Incidentally, the effort of trying to grip tightly and control the gun will tire you out if you have to do any sustained firing.

2. Lift the safety-catch towards you with your second fingers and,

3. Press in the thumb-piece with your thumbs.

Note 1. The raising of the safety-catch clears the way for the forward movement of the firing-lever. The safety-catch is kept in its normal, or down, position by means of a spring which also serves to keep the firing-lever to the rear. In the "down" position the safety-catch bars the way against any forward movement of the firing-lever sufficient to fire the round in the chamber.

Note 2. When the firing-lever goes forward, the pawl at the bottom pushes forward the bottom of the trigger bar lever. This, being pivoted in the centre, has its top portion withdrawn to the rear. The top of the trigger bar lever is engaged in front of a projection at the rear of the trigger bar. The trigger bar is thus pulled to the rear. At the front of the trigger bar is a slot in which lies the tail of the trigger. The backward movement of the trigger bar, therefore, draws back the tail of the trigger. The trigger is pivoted in the centre and thus its nose goes forward and is released from the bent of the tumbler. The semi-upright position of the tumbler prior to this has kept the firing-pin to the rear with the lock spring compressed. The tumbler now being free to rotate, the firing-pin is allowed to fly forward, under the influence of the lock spring, and fire the cap of the round in the chamber.

The above is a brief résumé of the action taking place up to the moment of firing of the first shot.

(iii) To unload.

1. Pull the crank handle back on to the roller and release it.
2. Repeat.
3. Disengage the top and bottom feed pawls by squeezing the pawl grips.
4. Keeping the pawls disengaged, as in 3 above, withdraw the belt.
5. Lift safety-catch and press thumb-piece.

Note. The pulling to the rear of the crank handle without any motion to feed the belt over for a round to be in position to be gripped by the extractor achieves the following results:

(i) The round in the chamber has been extracted and when the extractor drops, it either drops off of its own accord, or, when the extractor rises, it is forced off by the seating for ejection just underneath the bottom of the rear of the barrel.

(ii) The round in the feed block is withdrawn as usual, and put in the chamber, but no fresh round is gripped by the top of the extractor.

(iii) The round now in the chamber is disposed of as in (i) by the second rearward movement of the crank handle. The face of the extractor is thereby cleared of cartridges.

(iv) The belt has been held in position up till now by the bottom pawls lying behind the second round in the feed block and the top pawls behind the first round. The latter pawls feed the round into position as recoil takes place, while the former prevent any backward movement of the belt when the top pawls recover to their first position in readiness for feeding the next round.

The pawls must, therefore, be cleared out of the way before the belt can be withdrawn to the right.

SECTION IV

MACHINE CARBINES

1. .45-INCH THOMPSON MACHINE CARBINE.

MAGAZINE CATCH

(a) Particulars.

Service designation.	Thompson Machine Carbine.
Method of operation.	Projection of spent case.
Locked or unlocked at the moment of firing	Not locked, but on the other hand not in the same class as the simple "blow back" type of weapon. Breech opening is delayed by the adhesion of slipping inclined faces. (Blish system.)
Weight.	10 lbs approx.
Length.	33½ ins.
Capacity of magazine	Drum 50 rds. (obsolete). Box 20 rds.
Type of Fire.	Change lever for "single shot" or "auto."
Rate of fire.	600–700 r.p.m.
Type of sights.	Aperture.
Range of Adjustment.	0–600 yds.

(b) Loading and unloading.

(i) To fill magazines.

(*a*) DRUM TYPE. Remove the winding-key by lifting up the flat spring, thereby disengaging its stud from the centre piece, and sliding the key sideways out of engagement with the two slots on either side of the centre piece. Lift off the cover of the magazine. Fill by placing five rounds base downwards in between each claw of the rotor. Load up anti-clockwise and fill the outer spirals first. When it comes to the last compartment, position the rotor with one claw opposite the mouth of the magazine. Replace the cover with the slot in the side over the projecting stud on the bottom left half of the magazine. Slide on the winding-key making sure that the stud on the flat spring is correctly engaged in the centre piece. Wind clockwise nine clicks (or as otherwise indicated on the magazine).

(*b*) Box TYPE. Hold the magazine in the left hand, mouth uppermost, and base against the body. Place rounds singly on top of the platform or preceding round with the right hand, and press down into the magazine with the left thumb (i.e. as for hand filling of Bren thirty-round magazine).

(ii) To load.

(*a*) DRUM MAGAZINE. *Cock the weapon*. With the winding-key to the front, insert the two ribs of the magazine into the horizontal grooves in the front of the body from the left side. Force the magazine over to the right until the magazine-catch engages. The magazine can be put on from right to left, but forcing it home from this direction is liable to strain the magazine-catch.

N.B. The drum magazine cannot be put on the carbine when the moving parts are in the forward position. This is due to interference between the underside of the bolt and the magazine mouth.

(*b*) Box TYPE. *Cock the weapon*. Insert the rib on the back of the magazine in the corresponding recess in the body in front of the trigger-guard, and force upwards until the magazine-catch engages.

N.B. The box magazine can be put on when the moving parts are forward, i.e., with the carbine uncocked, but great care is necessary to ensure that the magazine-catch is engaged since the over draw of the magazine-spring has to be taken up before engagement is positive. This course is not recommended.

(*c*) Set change lever at "R" or "A" according to type of fire desired. R = single shot (repetition) and A = automatic.

N.B. The change lever can only be moved when the weapon it cocked.

(iii) To unload.

(*a*) To remove either type of magazine, press up the thumb-piece of the magazine-catch on the left side of the body and remove the magazine—drum type to the left, box type downwards.

(*b*) Press trigger and ease moving parts forward under control.

2. 9 mm. STEN MACHINE CARBINE.

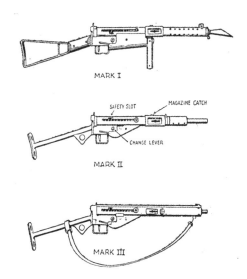

(a) Particulars.

Service designation.	Sten Machine Carbine. Mark I, II or III.
Method of operation.	Projection of spent case.
Locked or unlocked at. moment of firing	Unlocked. Simple blow-back action
Weight, without magazine.	Mark 1,8 lbs. Mark II, 6¾ lbs. Mark III, 6 lbs. 6 ozs.
Length.	Mark I, 35 ins. Mark II 30 ins. Mark III, 30 ins.
Magazine Type.	Box.
Capacity	32 rounds.
Weight filled.	1½ lbs.
Weight empty.	10½ ozs

Type of fire.	Single shot or automatic.
Rate of fire (cyclic)	500–550 rounds per minute.
Sights.	Fixed aperture backsight, barleycorn foresight (fixed range, 100 yds.).
Ammunition.	9 mm. All types of Parabellum and most other 9 mm. cartridges can be used in this weapon.

(b) Loading and unloading.

(i) To fill magazines.

Slip the filler on to the magazine, place the base of the magazine against the body and whilst working the filler lever with one hand place cartridges, base first, into the hollow of the lever with the other. Work the lever with a smart, firm movement.

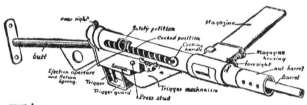

THE 'STEN GUN'

(ii) To load.

1. Insert the magazine in the magazine housing, and push home until you are certain that the magazine catch has engaged.

2. Pull back the cocking handle and, unless fire is to be opened at once, slip it into the safety slot.

Note. The breech-block should NEVER be left forward when a filled or partly filled magazine is in the carbine, since, if this is done and the weapon is jerked sharply, a round may be fired unintentionally.

3. Push change lever to Right for Single Shots (R) or to Left for Automatic (A).

(iii) To unload.

1. Grasp the magazine with the fingers of the left hand; press down the magazine catch with the left thumb, and at the same time withdraw the magazine from the housing.

2. Press the trigger and ease the breech-block forward under control.

4. 9 mm. SCHMEISSER MACHINE CARBINE.

(a) Particulars.

Method of operation.	Projection of spent case.
Locked or unlocked.	Unlocked. Simple blow-back action.
Weight.	9 lbs. 6 ozs.
Length.	33¼
Capacity of magazine.	32 rounds.
Type of fire.	Single shot or auto.
Rate of fire.	500–600 rounds per minute.
Type of sights.	Open.
Range of adjustment	100–1,000 metres.
Ammunition.	Parabellum type.

(b) Loading and unloading.

(i) To fill magazines.

Proceed as for the Thompson box magazine.

(ii) To load.

Insert mouth of magazine in magazine housing, and press home until the catch engages. Pull back the cocking-handle.

(iii) To unload.

Press in the magazine catch, which is situated on top near side of the magazine housing, and withdraw the magazine. Press the trigger.

5. GERMAN PARACHUTE TROOPS MACHINE CARBINE (Schmeisser Type).

(a) Particulars.

Method of operation.	Projection of spent case.
Locked or unlocked.	Unlocked. Simple blow back action.
Weight.	9 lbs.
Length.	25 ins. when butt is folded.
Capacity of magazine.	32 rounds.
Type of fire.	Automatic only.

Rate of fire.	500–540 rounds per minute.
Type of sights.	Open. Very thick blade foresight, and square notch backsight.
Range of adjustment	Two flip-up leaves calibrated for 100 and 200 metres.
Ammunition.	9 mm. Parabellum type.

(b) Loading and unloading.

As for Schmeisser.

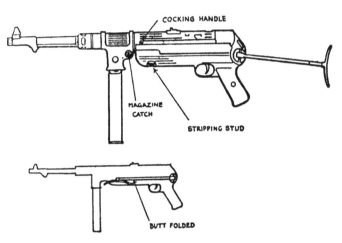

SECTION V

REVOLVERS AND AUTOMATIC PISTOLS

Preliminary.

The term "pistol" is used in the army as a general one, and is taken as meaning either a "revolver" or an "automatic pistol."

Any pistol, owing to the short length and the ease with which it can be pointed in any direction, is dangerous to both friend and foe alike if improperly handled. This dictum holds good even when it is being handled by an expert. In the hands of the fool or the man who knows little about it, it is much more likely to be dangerous to his comrades than to the enemy. For these reasons I make no apology for setting out below certain time-honoured precepts which should invariably be observed when handling pistols. The observance of these rules prevents accidents; neglect of them will one day lead to an accident and subsequent useless regrets.

The following rules must always be observed:

(i) Never leave a loaded pistol lying about where other people can get at it without your knowing about it.

(ii) When laying a pistol down, always "break" it or "open" it, if a revolver, or take out the magazine and clear the chamber if an automatic.

(iii) If you want to pick up someone else's pistol, never do anything with it until you have proved that it is unloaded. If it is loaded, unload it and kick the person who left it unattended the next time that you see him.

(iv) When dealing with an automatic, always remove the magazine first before you clear the chamber. If you do not do this and look at the chamber first, the unloading of the round in the chamber will certainly be accomplished, but the next round from the magazine will be fed in in its place. Subsequent removal of the magazine will not clear the round in the chamber. Neglect of this precaution causes more accidents with automatics than any other misdemeanour.

(v) If, despite all warnings, you have left your pistol lying about, always treat it as someone else's when you pick it up again – see (iii) above. Another person, just as careless as you are, may have picked it up and it may not be in the same condition as when you left it. It is better to be sure than sorry.

(vi) Last but not least, never point a pistol, whether loaded or unloaded, at anyone unless you mean business.

1. .455-INCH WEBLEY REVOLVER Mk. VI.

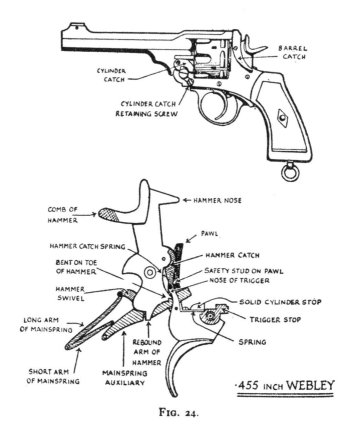

FIG. 24.

(a) Particulars.

Service designation.	Pistol No. 1.
Weight.	2 lbs. 6 ozs.
Length.	11¼ ins.
Length of barrel.	6 ins. Earlier Marks have shorter barrels. Target models 7½ ins.
Number of chambers.	Six.

Cylinder rotates.	Clockwise.
Ammunition	⎧ .455 inch Mk. II. For practice use only – lead bullet. ⎨ ⎩ .455 inch Mk. VI. For service use. This is nickel jacketted

2. .380-INCH PISTOL No. 2.

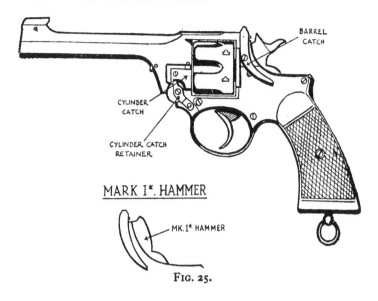

MARK I*. HAMMER

FIG. 25.

(a) Particulars.

Service designation.	Pistol No. 2 Mk. I and I*.
Weight.	1 lb. 11½ ozs.
Length.	9½ inches.
Number of chambers.	Six.
Cylinder rotates:	Clockwise.
Ammunition.	British .380 in.

Note. The Mark I pistol can be fired either by cocking or pulling through. The Mark I* will only function by double action, i.e. by pulling through. In the later mark the comb of the hammer and the bent of the hammer have been abolished.

There are two marks of butt grip, Mark I and Mark II. The Mark II grips are somewhat fuller than the Mark I and have grooves cut in them to accommodate the thumb and trigger finger respectively.

(b) Stripping and assembling.

(i) To strip.

1. Unscrew cylinder retainer fixing screw and remove cylinder.
2. Unscrew screw securing butt grips and remove grips.
3. Unscrew barrel catch screw and remove barrel catch.

Note. Before unscrewing, the tension should be taken off the screw by compressing the spring. Do not use pliers.

4. Unscrew body plate screws on left side (4) and remove plate.
5. Lever back the top of the pawl and lift out.
6. Unhook mainspring from the hammer swivel and remove spring.
7. Knock out mainspring auxiliary fixing pin and remove auxiliary.
8. Rotate hammer backwards and remove.
9. Take out trigger and safety stop.
10. Take out cylinder stop and spring.

(ii) To assemble.

Reverse the above order.

Note. When assembling the pawl, raise the mainspring auxiliary slightly, so that the latter rides on top of the pawl axis pin.

4. .450-INCH AND .455-INCH COLT AUTOMATIC PISTOLS.

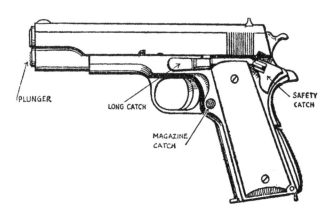

(a) Particulars.

Common names.	Colt .45 auto, and Colt .455 auto.
Weight:	
Loaded.	2 lbs. 11 ozs.
Unloaded	2 lbs. 6 ozs.
Length overall.	8½ ins.
Length of barrel	4¾ ins. including chamber.
Number of rounds in. magazine	Seven.
Ammunition.	.450-in. and 455-in. automatic (i.e. rimless). .455 will NOT fit .450 pistols, but the .450 may be fired in most .455 automatic weapons.
Locked or unlocked.	Locked.
Sights.	Fixed.

(b) Loading and unloading.

(i) To fill the magazine.

1. First withdraw the magazine from the pistol by pressing the spring catch on the left of the pistol just in rear of the trigger.

2. Holding the magazine in one hand place the base of each cartridge about half-way along the preceding one and then push down and back using both thumbs.

(ii) To load.

Push the magazine well home into the butt, pull back the moving portions as far as possible and allow them to return fully forwards. The pistol is now loaded and cocked.

(iii) To unload.

Remove the magazine. Pull the moving parts back sharply to eject the round in the chamber. Press the trigger.

Note. Always remove the magazine FIRST, and pull the moving portion back SECOND.

8. 9mm. BORCHARDT-LUGER (PARABELLUM) AUTOMATIC PISTOL.

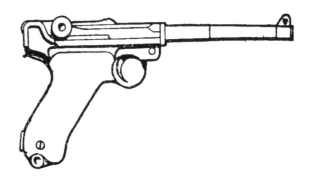

(a) Particulars.

Common name.	9 mm. Luger
Weight.	2 lbs.
Length.	8¾ ins.
Length of barrel.	3.9 ins.
Number of rounds in normal magazine	8 rounds.
Ammunition	9 mm. Parabellum. Mauser 9 mm. ammunition will NOT do.
Locked or unlocked.	Locked by toggle joint.

There is a longer type with a special holster. The latter can be fitted on to either the long or short pistols to serve as a butt for reasonably accurate shooting at distances in excess of normal pistol ranges.

(b) Loading and unloading.

(i) Loading.

1. Place the mouth of a full magazine in the magazine opening in the bottom of the butt, and press home until you hear or feel the magazine-catch engage.

2. Holding the butt of the pistol in the right hand, take hold of the two knurled knobs of the crank with the thumb and forefinger of the left hand, and pull smartly upwards and backwards, and then leave go of the crank. The above action will cock the weapon and at the same time the top round in the magazine will be fed into the chamber.

(ii) Unloading.

1. Remove magazine by pressing in magazine-catch, which lies on the left side of the pistol just behind the trigger.

2. Carry out the loading motion of pulling the crank back and letting it go. This will extract the round in the chamber and, since the magazine had previously been removed no other round will be fed in.

3. Release springs by pulling the trigger.

9. 7.63 MM. AND 9 MM. MAUSER AUTOMATIC PISTOL.

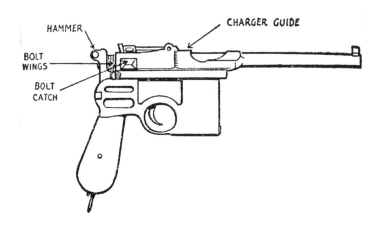

(a) Particulars.

Common name.	Mauser pistol
Weight.	2 lbs. 8 ozs.
Weight with wooden holster.	3 lbs. 10 ozs.
Length.	11 ins.
Length of barrel.	5½ ins.
Number of rounds. in magazine	10 rounds.
Ammunition	{ 7.63 mm. } Mauser { 9 mm. } Many, but not all, of the 9 mm. weapons will take Parabellum ammunition, as used in machine carbines.
Locked or unlocked.	Locked by rising link engaging bolt.
Type of sights.	Open.
Range of adjustment.	50–500 metres. In some cases the sight may be graduated to 600 or 1,000 metres.

This pistol is commonly found with a wooden holster which can be fitted as a butt and enables the weapon to be used for reasonably accurate shooting at distances greater than the normal range of pistols.

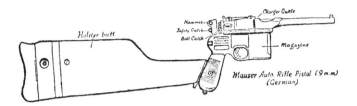

9mm Mauser automatic with the wooden holster attached as a butt.
From *Home Guard Officers & Section Leaders Handbook* by Alfred Kerr
(Hazell, Watson & Viney Ltd., September 1941)

(b) Loading and unloading.

(i) To load.

1. Pull back the bolt, by means of the ribbed wings at the back, to its full extent. This will cock the hammer and also allow the magazine platform to rise and prevent the bolt closing again on an empty breech.

2. Insert a charger into the guides in rear of the breech and push the rounds steadily into the magazine.

3. Remove the charger and the bolt will close carrying the first cartridge into the breech.

(ii) To unload.

1. Work the bolt backwards and forwards until it is held open by the magazine platform.

2. Holding the bolt back with one hand depress the magazine platform with the thumb of the other hand and ease the bolt forward, making sure no cartridge has been left in the breech.

3. Press the trigger.

Note. An alternative method, not to be recommended, is to remove the magazine base plate, spring and platform, when the rounds will fall out. It would then only be necessary to work the bolt once to clear the cartridge in the chamber, press the trigger and replace the magazine platform, spring and base plate.

10. 9mm. WALTHER MODEL .38 AUTOMATIC PISTOL (GERMAN).

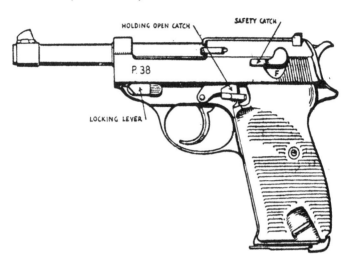

(a) Particulars.

Common names.	P.38, or 9mm. Walther auto.
Weight:	
Loaded.	2 lbs. 5 ozs.
Unloaded.	2 lbs. 2 ozs.
Length, overall.	8½ ins.
Length of barrel	4⅞ ins. including chamber.
Capacity of magazine.	8 rounds.
Ammunition.	9 mm. Parabellum.
Locked or unlocked.	Locked by rising block.
Sights.	Fixed.

(b) Loading and unloading.

(i) To fill magazine.

1. Withdraw magazine by pushing back the catch at the base of the pistol grip, when the magazine should spring out far enough to enable it to be gripped in the fingers.

2. Place the base of each round just in front of the magazine lips and press down and backwards into place.

(ii) To load.

1. Push magazine home into pistol grip.

2. Pull the slide back as far as possible and allow it to run forwards under the influence of the return spring.

Note. It does not matter whether the safety-catch is in the horizontal FIRE position or whether it has been turned down to the SAFE position. In the former case the weapon is now cocked and ready to fire, in the latter case the hammer will be in the fired position and to fire it will only be necessary to set the safety-catch to FIRE and press the trigger. It is NOT necessary to cock the hammer as this pistol has a "double action" hammer mechanism.

3. If the safety-catch is not at SAFE move it downwards into this position. This will release the hammer which will fly forward but will NOT fire the round in the chamber.

(iii) To unload.

1. Remove magazine.

2. With safety-catch in either position pull back the slide as far as possible to remove round from chamber and let it run forward.

3. If the safety-catch is set at FIRE move it to SAFE; this will release the hammer and thus ease the springs.

CHAPTER 7

HAND GRENADES

Hand grenades, along with all other munitions, were in very short supply in the aftermath of the Dunkirk evacuation and the Home Guard units had to make do largely with what they could improvise themselves in the early months. Molotov cocktails would have been the best that most units could have hoped to have at their disposal for some time although quantities of ST grenades, or sticky bombs, were also made available to the Home Guard. The latter was primarily an anti-vehicle weapon and would have had only limited use in an anti-personnel capacity. Once supplies of war materials became more plentiful, the No. 36 Mills bomb, the standard British Army fragmentation grenade, was made available to Home Guard formations. Careful training was required to use the No. 36 safely as, although the throwing range was around 30 yards, the danger area in which fragments could still kill or wound was about 100 yards.

The Home Guard Training Manual **(1942)**

HAND GRENADES

1. By far the most important weapon for close quarters fighting is the hand grenade. It has three good points.

(a) A short range.

(b) It can be thrown high in the air, and will then drop almost perpendicularly.

(c) It causes damage within quite a large area. This means that it is ideal for throwing from a ditch beside the road, or over a hedge, or over a barricade, or into a street from behind a wall or building, etc.

A well-trained strong man can throw a (No. 36) High Explosive grenade from twenty-five to thirty-five yards. It can be not only thrown over one's own cover, but it can be made to drop on an enemy behind the same sort of cover.

For example, a tank crew sheltering behind their tank can be driven away into the open, where they can be dealt with by rifle fire.

Of course, this means that the enemy can also drive you from your cover, if you permit them to find cover close enough to your own position. The probable danger area of a H.E. grenade is twenty yards in all directions from the point of burst; but fragments can inflict wounds up to at least one hundred yards.

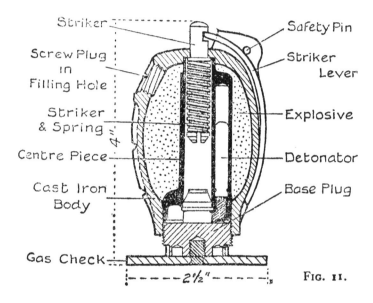

FIG. 11.

2. Description of H.E. Grenade. The outside is grooved so that when the grenade explodes it shall break easily into pieces. As shown in the diagram there is a striker lever fitted flush to the surface of the grenade, so that it shall not catch on anything as it is taken out of your knapsack. This lever is held in position by a safety pin.

The grenade is held firmly with the lever under the fingers, and when the moment comes to throw it, the safety pin is pulled out. So long as the lever is held, the grenade is safe; but when the grenade leaves the hand, the lever flies off, the striker is forced down on to the cap of the igniter set by the spring; and a fuse is lit, which will burn for seven seconds, at the end of which time the grenade explodes.

3. How to Throw. Grenades are thrown with the same arm action as that of an over-arm bowler at cricket. This enables you to propel them with a high trajectory, which is suitable for their purpose of attacking over obstacles such as barricades. As they are meant entirely for close-quarters fighting, there is no point in trying to throw them very far; it is much more important to get accuracy than length of throw.

It is important that every man should learn to throw the grenade with the movement which comes most natural to him. He must cultivate a free natural body swing rather than any set of drilled movements. During grenade practice you must make a point of accurately observing where the grenade falls. You will practise throwing over a high wire, and from behind cover, both standing and in a lying position. You will throw into circles marked on the ground, always remembering that you are throwing at an enemy who is behind cover.

Only one man will throw at a time. No man will throw without a direct order: grenades will never be thrown from man to man. No man will attempt to catch a grenade: no man will pick up a grenade which has been thrown, until ordered to do so.

These instructions must be rigidly obeyed, in order that, from the very start, you will instinctively learn to treat grenades with respect. There is no need to be nervous with a grenade, however, as long as you understand it.

4. Throwing practice with live grenades will only take place on a grenade range and under a qualified instructor as defined in Home Guard Training Instruction.

5. The following diagrams will make the nature of hand grenade practice perfectly clear to you.

EXERCISES

1. – Standing Position

1. Ready Position. Pick up a grenade. Hold it in the right hand, base downwards, the lever under the base of the fingers, the thumb just below the filling screw gripping it firmly. Place the first or second finger of the left hand through the ring of the safety pin – the hands with the knuckles uppermost and close to the waist. Face the target, turn to the right and balance the body by carrying off the left foot towards the target.

2. Prepare to Throw. Keeping the left arm still and close to the body, withdraw the pin (during practice go through the action of withdrawing the pin) by thrusting the right hand downwards and backwards. Glance at the shoulders of the grenade to see that the whole pin has been drawn out. Keep the pin until the grenade has been thrown.

FIG. 12.

FIG. 13.

3. Throw. Fix the eyes on, or in the direction of the target, keeping the left shoulder pointing at the target. Slightly bend the right knee. Swing back as far as possible, allowing the left arm (and foot if necessary) to come up naturally. Without pause swing quickly forward, keeping the right arm upright and deliver the grenade.

NOTE. When throwing in open country lie down at once after throwing to avoid fragments.

2. – Lying Position

1. Ready Position. Lie face downwards directly towards the target. Hold the grenade as in the standing position, both hands close under the chin, elbows outwards.

2. Prepare to Throw. Remove the pin as before.

3. Throwing. Place the hands in a natural position for pressing up, keeping the pin in the left hand. Press quickly up. Keeping the left knee on the ground, swing the body quickly back, allowing the left arm to come up and the right leg to go back naturally. Keeping the eyes and left shoulder on the line of the target, swing forward, right arm as upright as possible, and deliver the grenade. Observe the fall of the grenade. Quickly lie down.

CHAPTER 8

NIGHT FIGHTING

This chapter is taken from *The Art of Night Fighting – A Manual of Instruction for the Home Guard*, written by Alfred E. Kerr. Kerr served with the 1st Battalion, London Irish Rifles, a Territorial unit forming part of 1st London Infantry Brigade. Kerr was a prolific writer of training manuals, including *The Home Guard Officer's and Section Leader's Handbook* and *The Art of Guerrilla fighting and patrol*. Kerr, like a number of serving officers, based his writing on his personal experience and his advice often differed from the military orthodoxy. He held what he called "fireside theorists" in considerable disdain.

The Art of Night Fighting – A Manual of Instruction for the Home Guard (1943)

NIGHT FIGHTING

PATROL ESSENTIALS AND COMPOSITION

In dealing with the problem of patrols designed for guerrilla operation, especially those primarily intended for night operation, the Home Guard commander must bear in mind that he is confronted by many obstacles which do not affect his counterpart in the Regular forces. Chief of these is the age problem. Unlike the Army, the Home Guard officer has to reckon with the fact that a large proportion of his men are veterans – veterans in every sense of the word. Now, while such veterans could, because of their past experience, put up an even better showing against the enemy than many of our immature troops of recent vintage, yet in the matter of patrol fighting their age may, in many cases, affect their ability to perform this somewhat arduous undertaking.

Thus it behoves the commander to exercise great care in selecting the men to form these patrols, to choose only those volunteers sound in wind and limb, and also definitely above the average in mental standard. He should select men of initiative and resource and possessing no small measure of confidence in themselves. Further, they must be prepared to submit to a very rigid standard of discipline, and be capable of carrying out orders, however difficult, successfully and without question.

Provided always that the volunteer is physically sound and mentally alert, the more mature he is, the better will he be for this type of operation.

The choice of a section, or patrol, leader is a matter calling for special consideration. The virtues possessed by the members of the patrol must be magnified many times in the make-up of this person. It is imperative that he should have attained the highest standard of efficiency in ordinary military training, and, apart from possessing the utmost initiative and resource, should be capable of commanding, and holding, the complete confidence of his men. He must be able to give orders, clearly and explicitly, and see that they are carried out efficiently and without question.

In forming the sections, or patrols, for night fighting, it is suggested that the commander should compose one or more platoons of selected volunteers, even if it entails a reshuffle of an entire company. These patrol volunteers should then undergo intensive training in this type of operation, special emphasis being given in the curriculum to the work and conduct of night fighting and fieldcraft, generally.

It might not be possible to form and train a large number of patrols from the average company, but it should be possible to raise at least three or four patrols each of, say, nine men and a patrol leader.

In making the choice of the patrol leaders, selected men should be put through a course of guerrilla and patrol fighting. Instruction should be given in the art of using cover, journeying by night and day over open and wooded country, methods of stealthy approach, and training in the art of noiseless liquidation should also be included in this course. Those volunteers who show the greatest aptitude for, and intelligent assimilation of, the training given should be earmarked for the position of patrol leaders.

Apart from the individual training for the selected patrols, commanders, particularly those in outlying and country districts, should instruct all the men under their control in the general principles of night fighting. This is made necessary by the fact that the enemy is almost certain to precede any invasion of these islands by dropping advance airborne troops under cover of darkness. Such a threat to the national security must be met with ruthless vigour. Unless the men defending the territory are efficient in conducting operations at night, the only result must be a wanton waste of ammunition and an enemy who will have succeeded in establishing himself in positions from which it will take much trouble and loss of life to dislodge him.

Any operation undertaken in the darkness must be preceded by intelligent planning and close co-ordination by the units working in the area. It is imperative that plans should be formulated between the adjoining commands to prevent any possible mistaking of other friendly units for the enemy, or that the defenders disclose their positions to the enemy by endeavouring to establish the identity of other units so operating.

Later several suggestions will be given which should serve to overcome this, the greatest danger to successful conduct of night engagements.

While it must always be borne in mind that to attain the keynote of efficiency in a patrol or section all its members should be capable of taking over any of the key posts, even that of leader, if necessary. To facilitate speedy training it is suggested that the man in each patrol who shows the greatest aptitude and keenness should take over the post of first scout, then the next in order of merit the position of second scout or pivot. At the same time the remaining members should be encouraged to understudy their fellows in these posts.

When the patrol leader is considered sufficiently proficient in patrol operation, he should then be detailed to take over the training of his own section or patrol, and to school them in intensive practical patrolling over the particular stretch of territory allotted to his patrol. By this system, and by diligent study and logging of the characteristics of the countryside over which the unit will operate, the patrol will be able to take full advantage of cover and suitable positions from which to engage any enemy opposing them in the area.

Once the natural characteristics have been mastered, steps should be taken to prepare suitable hide-outs and ambush or defensive positions, and to make ready caches for the holding of ammunition or supplies, against the day of actual conflict. By so doing, the patrol will be in a position to match and successfully combat any attempt to land enemy in their own particular stretch of country.

EXERCISES FOR ACCURATE NIGHT FIRING

The problem of accurate small-arms fire at night is one on which many conflicting opinions are expressed. Some maintain that it is impossible to achieve any real degree of accuracy in darkness, others that it is a matter of individual intuition and an accomplishment given only to a few; but it can be greatly developed by systematic exercises and practice, and to this end a simple apparatus should be manufactured by the handymen of the unit themselves, to be utilised to very good effect.

But first let us take the problem of night fire in general, and the means necessary to achieve good results. In the matter of preparing for night fire from the light machine-gun it is possible, by fixing an aiming mark in the daytime, and if using a Bren or Lewis gun, to lock it in readiness for the night's fire after it has been sighted on the aiming mark, or on an objective. This is known as firing on "fixed line."

Aiming Marks

There are several ways in which an accurate aim can be assured when the gun is brought into play at night. One such method, if it is desired to cover a fairly distant objective, is to elevate and sight the weapon until it is approximately breast-high on anyone at that distance, and then lock the tripod in that position. A tripod is used on the Bren and Lewis for fixed line, instead of the bipod normally used when firing in the daytime. If it is likely that the gun's position is liable to be altered to serve some other emergency, an aiming mark consisting of a short piece of branch or stake, painted white, chalked, or stripped of its bark at one end, should be driven into the ground at a convenient distance from the gun, its white portion being of the required height to aim the gun to inflict casualties, judged in relation to a possible enemy position (fig. 1).

FIG. 1

Aiming marks can also be used to great advantage when firing from prepared defensive positions with small arms. If they are inserted in the ground at intervals a short distance in front of the position, they will ensure an accurate volume of fire at an approaching enemy. Their use is just as effective at night, for even in dense blackness the white portion remains visible. Sight the rifle on the aiming mark, then slowly swing it round to face your own field of fire.

Ambushes

Also, when preparing the setting for an ambush, care should be taken to fix an aiming mark for the light machine-gun, or for the riflemen if the former is not being used. The aiming mark will enable the machine-gunner and the riflemen to sight their rifles and maintain them at the ready, thus no movement will be necessary when the enemy body moves into the zone and thus attract his attention to the concealed party. It should be so placed on the opposite banking that its whitened end is on a level with a man's heart from the surface of the pathway along which the enemy party will be proceeding. At night, except in extreme darkness, this mark should be visible up to a distance of twenty to thirty feet. If there are trees near the ambush setting, a white patch chalked on the tree trunk at the requisite height will suffice instead of the stake (fig. 2). It is essential to give serious attention to these details, in order that the maximum effect is obtained from the first volley. This is necessary to ensure the success of the ambush and the safe get-away of the patrol undertaking the operation.

FIG. 2

The problem of accurate rifle fire in patrol engagements is rather more complicated, as there are no prepared positions from which to engage, save in the case of ambushes. Some means is therefore necessary to ensure that night marksmen put their fire to good purpose when they engage the attention of the enemy. The importance of such accuracy will be understood when it is explained that in patrol fighting it is quite possible the patrol will be engaging numbers greatly in excess of their own strength. The chief essential of patrol operations is surprise attack coupled with a standard of fire which will ensure the greatest number of casualties with the first volley. The aim, then, should be to render a second volley unnecessary, or at worst a final burst to clean up the survivors of the first volley.

It will be conceded that the accomplished marksman fires with a certain intuitive *feel* for aim when operating in conditions which preclude seeing his sights. This gift for feel is dependent for its success on muscle control. By intensive practice in aiming one can tell by the reaction of one's arm muscles just how the rifle is pointing. If arm and muscle exercises are maintained over a suitable period of training, then continued for a further period in conjunction with snap-aiming, it should be possible to *sense* when one *is* aiming correctly at a target, even if unable to see the sights.

PATROL RENDEZVOUS AND SUPPLY CACHES

This is primarily a manual on night operation, but in detailing instruction in the use of patrol rendezvous and caches for storing supplies it should be borne in mind that this is also a very important practice in *all* patrol work.

Patrols are often required to remain on offensive operation for many days at a stretch. Particularly would this be so in the event of the enemy landing troops in the secluded moorland and wooded areas of the south and south-east, such as in Sussex or Hampshire—for example, in that rugged and densely wooded region of Sussex known as the Ashdown Forest, or in the sparsely populated and moorland territory from Lewes or Bexhill, through the coast areas to the Thames Estuary, or that huge stretch of the New Forest acreage of Hants and Wilts.

Rendezvous and Hide-outs

Because of the prolonged nature of their duties, it is necessary for the patrol to select and prepare a rendezvous near to or in the centre of their patrolling area. This rendezvous is even more essential as a meeting-place or rallying-point for the patrol members to forgather after arduous operation or unforeseen separation in a night engagement. The natural characteristics of the place chosen should enable the patrol to bivouac there in concealment. It should be located in a small clearing in a wood or coppice or among thick gorse, preferably the former, if such wood or cover is available (fig. 25). Another excellent site for a rendezvous is a dried-up boundary dyke or stream that is overhung with brambles or tall hedgerows. This will ensure against the prying eyes of enemy observers' or aircraft. It is more than likely, too, that enemy patrols would skirt such a place, or even cross it, without being aware of its portent as a hiding-place. By scooping out dugouts in its banks, the patrol would have shelter and protection against the elements. In excavating such hide-outs, all trace of the excavation should be obliterated and all soil removed carefully from its proximity. A framework of latticed branches, interwoven with leaves and bracken, would suffice to hide the entrances from casual observation.

Stake marking position of dug-out.

FIG. 25

Caches

As the patrol can only carry a limited supply of stores, etc., caches must be dug to contain replenishments of both ammunition and food. These caches are small pits sufficiently large in size to hold four packs each. Besides the caches necessary to hold the packs of the entire patrol, other caches must be prepared to house spare ammunition and grenades. First a hole must be excavated, and the soil carried away from the near vicinity. The hole should be large enough to accommodate four packs, two below and two on top. Choose a place that is dry and sandy, so that no water is likely to seep into the cache from the surrounding ground. After the sides have been levelled, line the sides of the cache with small thin branches, stuck vertically into the ground. By interleaving these branches with fronds of bracken or dry leaves and brush, a dry receptacle is in readiness to contain these valuable supplies. The supplies themselves can be stored inside biscuit tins, with tight-fitting lids. Ammunition boxes covered with waterproof material or groundsheets should suffice to keep these valuable articles dry and fit for use. The cover for the cache should consist of a. stout framework of branches, treated in the same manner as the insides of the cache.

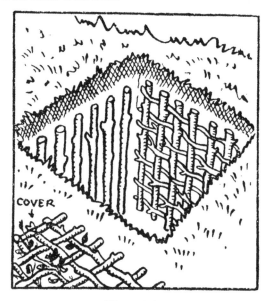

FIG. 26

The position of the rendezvous, and caches should, so far as is practicable, lie located near the centre of the patrolling area. This will enable the patrol to frustrate any landing attempts with the minimum of delay. In order that the rendezvous can be located without difficulty in the dark, its position should be logged, and all routes to it memorised by the patrol members. It is important, too, that the flanking patrols should be aware *of* its position in order that communication can be maintained at all times. When the patrol has bivouacked for the night, sentries must be posted. These should operate in pairs, and should be so sited that they can observe all approaches without moving from, concealment. If anyone approaches the post, one sentry will quietly wake the patrol, the other keep the intruder under constant observation.

SOURCES

INTRODUCTION

Penny Summerfield & Corinna Peniston-Bird, *Contesting Home Defence: Men, women and the Home Guard in the Second World War* (Manchester University Press, 2007)

CHAPTER 1

Major John Langdon-Davies, *The Home Guard Training Manual* (John Murray & The Pilot Press, 1942)

CHAPTER 2

Major John Langdon-Davies, *The Home Guard Training Manual* (John Murray & The Pilot Press, 1942)

CHAPTER 3

John Brophy, *Home Guard Drill and Battle Drill* (Hodder & Stoughton, 1943)

CHAPTER 4

John Brophy, *Advanced Training for the Home Guard* (Hodder & Stoughton, 1941)

CHAPTER 5

J. A. Barlow, 'Rifles and Rifle Shooting', in *The Home Guard Training Manual* by Major John Langdon-Davies (John Murray & The Pilot Press, 1942)

CHAPTER 6

Brigadier J. A. Barlow and Lt.-Col. R. E. W. Johnson, *Small Arms Manual* (John Murray, 1960)

CHAPTER 7

Major John Langdon-Davies, *The Home Guard Training Manual* (John Murray & The Pilot Press, 1942)

CHAPTER 8

Alfred E. Kerr, *The Art of Night Fighting – A Manual of Instruction for the Home Guard* (The Syndicate Publishing Co. Ltd., 1943)

Sources for chapters 1–8 were obtained from the library of the Royal Armouries Museum, the UK's national collection of arms and armour. Royal Armouries has one of the largest arms and armour reference libraries in the world, with special collections of early fencing books and military manuals, and an archive containing over 500,000 items from the 13th century onwards.